# ORANGE COUNTY
## THE DARK SIDE

*First Edition.*
Published March 2023
by Indies United Publishing House

Available in E-Book, Paperback, and Hardcover.

ISBN: 978-1-64456-592-6 [Hardback]
ISBN: 978-1-64456-593-3 [Paperback]
ISBN: 978-1-64456-594-0 [Mobi]
ISBN: 978-1-64456-595-7 [ePub]

Library of Congress Control Number: 2023931667

INDIES UNITED PUBLISHING HOUSE, LLC
P.O. BOX 3071
QUINCY, IL 62305-3071
indiesunited.net

# ORANGE COUNTY
## THE DARK SIDE

## CHRISTOPHER CURTIS

INDIES UNITED PUBLISHING HOUSE, LLC

# PROLOGUE

On October 29, 2002, walking through a hallway into the living room of the suite I rented, I thought to myself, *can't believe I am staying in this hotel for the second night in a row. I'm pressing my luck. I've gotta get out of Anaheim.*
I was staying with a girl named Tina, who I met a few days before with my homeboy. We started hanging out and I figured she was alright. Tina was good at making money with checks and things of that nature. So we had something in common. Who doesn't like to make money? Plus Tina was nice to look at with a friendly smile.

The Portofino Inn & Suites is a decent hotel in a Gang infested part of Anaheim about a mile away from Disneyland. The suites, with a living room, bedroom, and bathroom, could be a nice apartment if it had a kitchen. In my bedroom, on the dresser was a Pocket Tech digital gram scale and numerous 4.5x3, 4x4 and 2x2 inch bags - in the top drawer was also a gram of meth on a plate. In the living room, on the coffee table was a Fuji 35mm camera, a nylon pouch with numerous varied identification cards, Docu Seal 40 Laminator, and Photo Smart

130 printer. A large plastic container with bank statements, birth certificates, saving bonds, and blank checks sat on the floor.

"Chris, be back in a few hours; I have to take a couple of bank statements and checks to my friend," Tina explained.
"Okay, take the key card on the table. I won't be here when you return. Don't open the door for anyone, and remember, do not tell no one where I'm, staying."

"I won't Chris, stop trippin!" Tina walked out the door without another word.

I had just finished weighing out several bags of meth. Five separate ounces, four quarter ounces, and few grams for a friend. I had to deliver all this dope and get back here to meet my drug connection before 10 PM I wanted to be on my way back to Lake Havasu, Arizona before the sun rose in the morning. I'd been having terrible feelings that something bad was going to happen.

I placed all my dope in my little black bag, grabbed my cell phone, put my Glock 45 handgun down my pants, picked up my backpack, and headed for the front door. Before opening it, I looked through the peephole to make sure the coast was clear. With my hand under my shirt, holding my gun, I opened the door and stepped into the hallway outside of my room. I looked from one end of the hallway to the other. Feeling at ease, I slightly relaxed and headed for the underground parking garage.

As I stepped into the garage, I placed my hand back on my gun until I scanned the parking lot, looking for any hinky individuals. There was no one around just a whole bunch of empty parked cars. I headed for the Ford Explorer I rented the day before. As I was opening the door, a family obviously on vacation, was driving towards me, trying to locate a parking spot. I climbed inside the Ford, placed my backpack on the passenger seat, gun on my lap, and started the car. As I drove up the ramp into the ground floor parking lot tourists filled the parking lot. The full moon lit up the sky and I was starting to feel much better. All those terrible feelings I was having about something bad occurring had stopped.

I lit a smoke as I drove through the lot towards the main street. When I arrived at Harbor Boulevard, I looked both ways. The traffic was thick. I made a right onto Harbor; then when I got to Convention Way, I U-turned back towards Katella. I made a right on Katella going east. When I arrived at a red light there was a police car on my right in the far right-hand lane on Lewis Street. The police shined his spotlight on me, so I made a right on Lewis and a quick left into a gas station. All of a sudden, unmarked police cars raced into the gas station, practically surrounding me.

I looked from one officer to another thinking *Son of a bitch, I've got 2 -strikes, a Glock on my lap, a grip of meth, and four police officers staring at me through their windshields.* I hesitated, then pushed my gas pedal to the floor. There was just enough room for me to drive through the patrol cars, barely missing hitting one.

I went right back onto Katella eastbound, not slowing down for much. I wove in and out of traffic at high speed. I was careful as possible not to hit another car because if I did, I would certainly catch a life sentence then. I knew I had to dump the drugs and gun. I ditched the rent-a-car in the back of an apartment complex. Barely stopping the car, I grabbed my backpack, gun and hit the emergency brake, jumping out before it fully stopped. I dashed for the first fence I saw, hopping it into an unknown backyard.

I heard the police helicopter speeding toward my location. The backyard where I landed had a swimming pool. I started dumping bags of meth in. Before I finished I heard footsteps and officers yelling, "He went over the wall!" So I jumped back up and ran through the yard, leaping the next fence, and landing in front of a pit bull. I quickly turned around and jumped back the same way I came. I crossed the yard, hopping the next wall into the neighbor's backyard. As soon as my feet hit the ground, the police helicopter searchlight lit up the sky, extinguishing all hopes of my getaway. I ran through the next backyard and threw what little dope I had left in my possession. Unfortunately, I still had the Glock 45; I had to think quickly. I climbed onto a brick wall and started walking, one foot in front of the other to keep my balance.

As I walked along the wall I saw a tree overlapping it. As soon as the police helicopter's spotlight didn't shine directly on me, I balanced my gun on a tree branch, jumped off the wall and started running again. I came to a gate, opened it and RAN! As I turned the corner, I ran right into seven police officers, all screaming the same thing, "GET THE FUCK ON THE GROUND! NOW! DOWN!"

Looking down the barrel of their guns, with nowhere else to run, I got face down on the ground. SON OF A BITCH!

# CHAPTER 1

In 1980 at nine years of age, I was too full of energy. They called it ADHD or Attention Deficit Hyperactivity Disorder. No matter what you call it, one effect is an excess of energy that needs to be used on something. For me, it was running the streets, or should I say down the streets, of Orange County. I'd grab my backpack, filled with necessities for the day. I was out for the whole day and wouldn't be home until the street lights came on. In the early 80s, that was the deal most parents made with their kids. My parents were glad to get rid of me for the day. In my backpack was a flashlight, some food, maybe a pocketknife, and I was out of the house before my parents woke up.

Growing up on Morningside Street in the City of Orange, my best friends were Ricky and Erik. They were twin brothers. We'd been friends for the better part of 5 years. We did everything together. Our favorite thing was to ride our bikes through the storm drains under the streets. We'd ride those tunnels until there was no place else to ride.

By age 11, riding through pitch-dark storm drains was

exciting and scary all at the same time. The entrance to the storm drains was in the orange grove, directly behind my house. All three of us would snake our way to the entrance, arguing about who would go first this time.

See, whoever went first through the tunnels cleared the cobwebs for the rest of us. So nobody wanted to volunteer to lead the way.

"Ricky, your brother went first last time, come on," I explained.

"No way Chris! You go first." Ricky cried.

Erik looked over at me with suspicious eyes and said, "Have you ever gone first, Chris?"

"Of course I've gone first. You guys don't remember."

The twins looked back and forth at each other, confused. So before they could say anything else, I came up with a solution. "Let's draw straws. Whoever picks the smallest straw goes first."

"Well Chris, I don't know," Ricky muttered.

"Come on! Are we gonna argue all day about this?"

Finally we agreed to pick straws as soon as we got there. After drawing straws, we duct-taped our flashlights to the handlebars of our bikes. That time Ricky led the way. Once again I lucked out. Soon as we were all ready, we walked our bikes down into the drainage ditch.

You couldn't ride side by side inside the tunnels; there wasn't enough room. So we went one in front of the other. The further you rode into the tunnel, the smaller the light got behind you until you could no longer see the entrance light. I never admitted it, but I always had this awful feeling water would come rushing down the tunnel and wash us all away. The only light was our flashlights, other than the occasional storm drain. Every time you passed under a street inside the tunnel, there was always a storm drain.

We'd take advantage of the light at a storm drain and eat lunch. Being kids, we always made a big deal about riding the tunnels. Like it was the adventure of a lifetime. This tunnel ended in Villa Park, right at the entrance of the catwalk, across the street from Cerro Villa Junior High School.

I'd get back home all muddy and tired. Mom would make me take a bath, feed me, and I'd fall asleep as soon as I started watching television. I remember denying that I had fallen asleep.

"Son, go sleep in your room."

"I wasn't sleeping dad. I just had my eyes closed."

"Don't argue with me son."

On plenty of occasions I stumbled to my room, half asleep, hearing the M*A*S*H theme music ending.

The house on Morningside was full of good memories. We had a real pinball machine called "The Swinger." All the kids in the neighborhood were dying to come over and play pinball. We even had Intellivision, a popular video game. All this was around the time Devo (the group with the funny hats) came out. Briefly, life was good for my family.

I spent a lot of time at The Regal Lanes Bowling Alley, especially during the summer months. My brother Jay and I would get five dollars from Mom and race down to the bowling alley. We loved playing Space Invaders, Donkey Kong, and Asteroids, the most popular games at that time. Five dollars went quickly: an Icee and twenty video games were pretty much all we could get. Depending on how well you played those video games, time passed quickly. After the money was gone, I was back on my Diamondback bicycle, racing through the streets.

I was a Ritalin kid. In the 80s, if you were hyperactive like me, you were put on Ritalin. I vaguely remember the way Ritalin made me feel. I do remember being uncomfortable around other kids. I felt like I was always being looked at. It sure didn't improve my situation when every day at 11 AM, I was called out of class to take my medication. I felt out of place and to be honest, a little embarrassed. I don't remember being teased or anything like that; growing up was just sort of a blur.

As a kid I was constantly getting myself injured. One time dad took my brother Jay and me out of school for the day to go up to Big Bear to play in the snow. We were all bobsledding down this big hill. We would slide down the hill, but it didn't seem quite fast enough. So each time, we went higher and higher. I decided to go all the way to the top.

"Watch this!" I yelled as I gave myself a push and started my run down the hill. Everything seemed to be going alright until I hit a bump, flew of the sled, and slid down the rest of the hill on my side. It hurt like hell!

When I finally reached the bottom, I went straight to my dad's truck. I was in some serious pain. Later my dad came to check on me. As soon as I pulled my snowsuit off, dad started yelling, "Jay, grab all of our stuff. We're going to the hospital!"

I must've hit a rock because the left side of my leg was ripped open, just below my hip. Fatty tissue was actually hanging out of my wound. We spent the rest of that day in the hospital, having my leg stitched up. I remember that day vividly. The doctor had to cut away all the fatty tissue to close the wound. The pain was so intense I was screaming. That was just one of many incidents that would land me in the hospital over the years.

When my parents went out for the evening, Martin, Ricky and Erik's older brother, would babysit Jay and me. Then when my parents actually split, Derik, Martin's friend, would show up. Martin and Derik were really cool. Both were about sixteen. We never had a dull moment when my parents went out for the night. We lived behind an orange grove on Morningside, and when the sun went down, we'd throw oranges at cars driving down Orange County Avenue. Usually it was always the same outcome. Orange hits car, car screeches to a stop, and we run like hell back to our house, jumping the fence right into our backyard. We never were caught and every time Martin came over to babysit, that was our normal activity.

One night we're throwing oranges at cars and blam! We heard a car screech to a stop. This time however, we hit a police car. Red & blue flashing lights immediately lit up the night sky, and bright spotlights soon followed, scanning back and forth into the orange grove, trying to locate us.

Martin yelled, "Chris, Jay, run as fast as you can back to the house!"

We both ran as fast as our little legs would let us. My heart was pounding in my chest. Derik was right behind me.

"Go! Go!" He urged, practically pushing me. We made it back as fast as we could, jumped the fence and fell down laughing in the backyard. We were laughing and scared all at the same time. After we caught our breath, we went to the front yard to sit on the lawn. As soon as we sat down a police car came cruising down the street and stopped directly in front of the house.

Derik whispered, "Let me do the talking."

As the cop stepped out of his car, my dad pulled up with one of his buddies. Most nights when my parents went out for the evening, they went to "Marty's" a bar about five minutes away from the house. Dad got out of his truck, obviously a little tipsy and asked, "Officer, is there a problem here?"

"Yeah, around ten minutes ago one of my patrol cars was struck in the windshield by an orange, and it shattered the window." The cop replied, staring straight at us the whole time.

My dad looked at us for a second, then back at the cop and calmly said, "Well, officer, I was on the phone with my babysitter fifteen minutes ago and told him to wait out front for me because I was coming home for a few minutes. Martin, was Chris and Jay with you the whole time in the house?"

"Yes Mr. Curtis. We all were in the house." Replied Martin.

"There you have it officer; it couldn't of been these boys."

The cop was so furious that his face was visibly red. He gave us all a dirty look, jumped into his patrol car and left. Dad looked at us and just burst out laughing, then turned and went into the house with his friend.

My family seemed perfect at this time. Dad owned a company called "Curtis Masonry," and it was thriving and successful. Because of this, my brother and I had it good.

Christmas was exciting for us. I can't recall anything we didn't have on Morningside St. We'd wake up Christmas morning, tear open all of our presents, and drive to our grandparents' house to open more gifts. Grandma Iris (Dad's mother) was my favorite. She was always good to us.

Christmas Eve was nice as well. We usually went to my Aunt Maggi's house. She's my mom's sister who lived in Mission Viejo, located in South Orange County. Aunt Maggi is by far my favorite relative on my mom's side of the family. The whole family on mom's side would show up for Christmas Eve. All of us kids would play on the pool table and we ate a huge delicious turkey dinner. Those times are difficult to forget because they are precious memories.

Around the beginning of the fifth grade, my family started falling apart. Mom blamed it on dad, and dad blamed it on mom. Over the years I figured out on my own what really happened. I realized the start of the problems when my friend at the beginning of school asked, "Chris, why didn't your parents buy you new school clothes?"

I thought to myself, *School clothes? I don't have school clothes.* My only concern in the fifth grade was how long my bicycle would last. Because my bikes never seemed to last long. "What are you talking about Brian?"

"Look at everyone Chris. They're all wearing new school clothes, and you're still wearing the clothes from last year."

I looked at Brian confused and replied, "Whatever Brian, I don't care."

Mostly wealthy kids attended "Serrano Elementary" since it was located on the border of Villa Park. All the kids were wearing 501 blue jeans and polo shirts. I still wore the clothes from the year before.

I do remember asking my mom about clothes when I arrived home that day. "Mom, when am I going to get new school clothes?"

She gave me a concerned look and said, "We'll go next week honey."

Mom was probably shocked I even asked for new school clothes. Our situation became worse when my dad's construction company was sued. Dad had hired an outside company to build an elevator shaft because his company was too busy. The company he hired mixed the cement improperly and the elevator shaft imploded, causing thousands of dollars in damage, which my dad was responsible for.

To make matters worse, I discovered that my dad had a cocaine problem. Couple that with the recession, and there you have the devastation to our lives, which resulted in dad selling our home on good old Morningside St.

I recall explaining to Ricky and Erik that I was moving, and at that age it's difficult to leave your friends behind. We were packed and gone a week later.

# CHAPTER 2

Our new house, a rental, was right down the street so to speak. Far enough that I still had to change schools, but close enough to ride my bike to Regal Lanes.

The Clash, (my favorite band at that time) had just came out with their new album, "Combat Rock," and MTV was just becoming popular. Our house was right off Katella Ave, on Rueben Circle. It was a big house, two stories, four bedrooms, and a nice backyard. The best part was my new school was right across the street. All I had to do to get to Katella Elementary was jump my backyard wall and walk across Katella Ave., jump the chain link fence and I was on the playground. This was the last year anything would be normal for my brother and me. I remember walking to school on my first day. I was nervous, strung out on Ritalin, and shaking from the side effects. Even if I knew people, I still felt uncomfortable around them. Ritalin turned me into a tweaker at a young age; I just never realized it then.

In the parking lot on the way home from school I ran into this kid who asked, "Hey, what's your name? My name is

Timmy."

I looked around to see who he was talking to, and realizing he was talking to me, I replied, "My name's Chris."

"I haven't seen you around here. Are you new at the school?"

"Yeah, I just moved here a few weeks ago. I live in the cull-da-sac around the corner."

"You must've just passed me on the way to school because I live right across the street from a cull-da-sac."

I found out that Timmy lived only a minute away from my house. We became friends quickly. As the days passed, I met more and more kids, and thankfully, my first day of school was an all around success.

In no time I was all around the neighborhood. I began staying overnight at Timmy's house on the weekends. It wasn't long before I forgot all about my friends on Morningside St.

At home things were becoming increasingly worse. I remember waiting for my dad to come home on Friday nights so he could take me to race my bike. The YMCA held races every Friday night, and racing BMX bikes was all I wanted to do at eleven years old. I was impatient all week, waiting for Friday to arrive so I could race my bike.

I'd wait in the garage dressed in my racing gear, watching for my dad to drive around the corner. All week he would promise to take me racing, but when he arrived home on Friday, all I heard was the same old excuse, "I'm tired son. We'll go next weekend."

Thinking back then, my perception of his excuse sounded more like he just wanted to sit around and snort up the rent money and screw taking me anywhere. That's how it sounded in my head every time he made an excuse.

A few times, we did go racing. I never placed lower than second place, and ironically, I didn't get to go practice like the rest of the kids who raced.

I started spending most of my time with Timmy after school. Marie and Terry were always around too. Timmy was nothing like Ricky and Erik. Timmy was pushy; some might say bossy which I wasn't used to. Marie however was really nice. She was taller than me back then, but who wasn't at that time in my life. So it wasn't really a big deal. She always smelled so nice.

Terry on the other hand was a troublemaker, always pressuring us into doing stupid things we didn't want to do. Walking home from school with her became a dreadful experience even though it was only a short walk.

Unfortunately my new found friendship with them didn't last very long. After school we'd meet up in front of the school office and walk home together. One day when I went out to meet them I discovered they had left without me. I noticed them crossing Katella Avenue, so I ran to catch up. I caught up right in front of Timmy's house. When I reached them I noticed they all had odd expressions on their faces. I asked, "Why didn't you wait for me?" They looked from one to the other. Uncomfortabe no one wanted to answer. Finally Terry, with a stuck up little attitude said, "You're a cocaine sniffer, and we don't wanna be around you no more!"

"What're you talking about?" I replied.

Timmy spoke up and said, "We all know about your family and why you moved here. My parents told me everything Chris. Your family moved here because you're all cocaine sniffers, and you're not allowed at my house no more."

Marie didn't say anything. I could tell she felt bad for me.

"Let's get away from this cocaine sniffer." Terry remarked with venom in her voice. Then they walked away, leaving me standing there in utter shock, wondering what just happened.

By the time I made it to my front door, my eyes had tears in them. I couldn't believe what I heard. New friends accusing me and my whole family of being drug addicts is not something an eleven-year-old kid takes lightly.

As I walked through my front door, I threw my backpack down on the living room floor, and sat down heavily on the couch, tears streaming down my young face. My mother walked into the living room and saw how upset I was and asked, "What's wrong Chris?"

"All my friends are calling me a cocaine sniffer, and said we moved here because of dad, and that he has a cocaine problem."

My mother was stunned hearing this, and tears began to roll down her cheeks.

"Is it true mom? Does dad use cocaine?"

"No honey. Don't listen to those kids!"

Reflecting on those parts of my childhood is rough but what occurred over the next couple of weeks at school was even rougher. The embarrassment caused by everyone in school thinking you snort cocaine was too much for a fifth grader to deal with and it didn't work out too well for me.

I dreaded going to school. All the kids were calling me a drug addict and no one wanted to be around me. Instead of walking home like I used to, I would jump the wall into my backyard.

One day I was kicking around a soccer ball at recess time alone and this kid Bryce walked up and started talking to me Bryce was a half-Indian kid, and his long hair showed his Indian descent. Suddenly I had a new friend. Bryce lived in the same neighborhood just off Quincy St. He lived with his grandparents. His parents were divorced, and his mom was always moving around. It was good to have a new friend and we got along well.

Unfortunately, in a few weeks I was told we were moving again. I was actually relieved to be moving out of that house on Rueben Circle.

We moved to a house off Sacramento Street, with the 55 freeway right behind our house. It was not a nice house; it was pretty run down. There was more dirt than grass on the lawn. The house's green paint had seen better days and was peeling off in some areas. The backyard looked like a hurricane had swept through it the night before we moved in. The only seemingly good thing about the house was that at least it was in the same neighborhood, which meant I was still close to where Bryce lived.

At this time, I was twelve years old. Summer was

approaching and I was happy to be away from Timmy and the rest of the kids on Rueben Circle. In their eyes, my dad being a drug addict made me one too, making me uncomfortable around their judgmental stares. I was really glad to move away in fact, I felt great.

During the summer my parents spent a lot more time at Marty's bar and were arguing all the time.

Summer ended and marked the start of a new school year. Katella Elementary, had budget issues and the school was forced to close. We were all re-routed to Villa Park Elementary, which was a huge change for all of us. The kids at Villa Park Elementary were well dressed. Bryce and I weren't and the kids looked at us like we were bums; we could care less.

We met a new kid named Will, who started running around with us. Will lived on Adams St, the next street over from Bryce's grandma's. We all became good friends over time.

Not long into the school year my parents split up. My brother Jay and I went to live with my mom's sister. That only lasted about a week simply because there was no room for all of us. My mom rented an apartment near Glassell Avenue. Again this meant changing schools. I was really getting sick of having to meet new kids.

The new school was Taft Elementary and the first day was awful. It was 1984 and Van Halen had just released their album titled "1984." I had grown my hair long like Bryce, well, as long as my mom would allow. My friends and I wore Iron Maiden T-shirts, jeans with holes, and our newly grown long hair. The other kids, by comparison, wore new 501 jeans and Alligator polo-shirts; the yuppie style was emerging. Needless to say my friends and I did not fit in with the popular crowd. I stopped going to my new school pretty much after the first day. Instead I would hang out on the railroad tracks all day and when I'd see the other kids walking home from school, I'd head for home too. It lasted about a week before the school called my mom, who was not too thrilled about my behavior. I had stopped taking Ritalin and I couldn't really keep still. My life had turned upside down within a year.

A few nights later, my dad came over to pick up my brother and I for a visit. He brought his new girlfriend, surprising us because he and mom had only been separated for a month. He was already with someone new who was nowhere near as pretty as my mom. Of course I am biased, she is my mom and no one is prettier.

Jay and I were waiting out front of the apartment when dad drove up with the new lady, and I remember being nervous about meeting her. Dad hollered as he drove up, "Kids! This is Pauline, my new girlfriend."

Jay and I said "hi" politely but neither of us was enthusiastic about the whole ordeal and I'm pretty sure we made that evident.

Pauline was ten years younger than my dad. She had curly black hair and dark skin. The fact she was Italian was unmistakable.

Dad took us to a pizza place where we talked about how things were going for us. We learned Pauline listened to most of the same music as we did. Bands like: Led Zeppelin, The Cars, and of course, Pink Floyd. She also told us that she had a five-year-old kid named David.

After eating we went by dad's place on Sacramento St. and discovered that he had a new roommate named Joey, also Italian. Jay and I felt weird about all this. Joey seemed cool but looked really tough. We were talking for a few moments when the phone rang. Joey immediately went to another room to answer it. I didn't think much of it at the time except that it was strange, when he could've answered the phone five feet away in the kitchen. Later that night dad was talking to my brother and dad seemed sad. As I listened to them talk, I could vaguely hear dad asking questions about mom. I knew he was trying to win her back. I couldn't totally make out the conversation. Looking around that house I felt sorry for him. The house was run down. Compared to what we were used to. It just made me feel bad for my dad.

By the time I started seventh grade my mom was struggling and eventually lost our apartment. Dad wasn't helping matters as he wouldn't pay child support. Mom could not bring herself to go on welfare so we ended up living with dad.

When we moved in with dad, Pauline and her son David were already there. The first few days seemed strange for Jay and I, which would change fairly quickly as we learned.

Not even a week had passed since we moved in when we had a situation. I had just got home from school. Dad and Jay were sitting at the dining room table. The kitchen was connected to the dining room that had a sliding glass door that opened into the backyard. Most of the time the door stayed closed to shut out all of the noise from the 55 freeway, as well as the dust and exhaust fumes.

I noticed two packs of Marlboro cigarettes and two lighters sitting in front of Jay on the dining room table. He looked pretty confused at that moment.

Dad was sitting opposite Jay and said, "Chris, you're just in time. Come over here and sit down next to your brother, I want to explain something to the both of you." I gave Jay a dirty look because I knew the smokes weren't mine and I thought I was in trouble for something he did.

But dad shocked us both with what he had to say.

"While I was pulling your laundry from the dryer I discovered a cigarette lighter. I know it's not mine because you both know I use a Zippo lighter. So if your gonna smoke boys, I don't want you hiding it from me. Here is a pack of smokes for each of you."

He left us there speechless and in total shock without saying another word to either of us. At that time we thought it was the coolest thing in the world, our dad letting us smoke. Our house became the hangout spot from that day forward.

# CHAPTER 3

What happened the following New Year's Eve changed me and my friends' lives forever.

I met this kid named Jed, who lived about seven houses down the block. He was a really good kid in all respects. He was on the wrestling team, and the only thing I could see that seemed a little off was that he seemed a little shy or depressed. After learning that his dad had passed away, I understood why. Jed was always respectful, and we quickly became close friends.

On New Year's Eve, we were all listening to one of Pauline's records on my dad's stereo system in the dining room.

The Cars were playing in the background, and the song was "My Best Friend's Girlfriend." We must've played that same song 5 or 6 times. The house had people coming and going all night. It was kind of like a party situation but nobody stayed long.

Next to the dining room table was an entertainment system, and next to the sliding glass door was a hutch, given to my mom by one of her family members. In the past few months I noticed the walls becoming yellow from all the smoking going on in the house. Pauline had lost her job and instead of the house getting cleaner, it got dirtier. You would think it would be the opposite, but it wasn't.

At some point dad came walking into the room we were in and asked if we were having fun. We told him we were. He sat down at the table with us and pulled out a paper bundle from the pocket of his flannel shirt. Then he pulled out a straw and a razor blade. Jed and I exchanged a look of confusion. We literally had no clue as to what he was doing. Unfortunately, we would soon find out because he dumped the contents of the paper bundle onto the table and proceeded to chop the white stuff into a fine powder. This brought to mind something Timmy said about dad being a cocaine sniffer. Seeing what he was doing confirmed the fact that dad used drugs.

He continued to chop up the stuff and finally made three lines of powder on the table. I was pretty scared at this point. There were so many thoughts racing through my mind. At first I thought dad was teasing us or something. Worst of all, my heart was pounding right out of my chest. Jed wasn't fairing any better by the looks of him.

"Come try this son." Dad beckoned to me.

"What is it dad?" I asked timidly.

"It's coke son. Don't worry; it's not going to hurt you."

As I rose to my feet I thought my dad was going to start laughing like he was only playing a joke but no laughter came, not even a hint of a joke. I walked around the table to where he was sitting.

Again he assured me I wouldn't get hurt and that he wouldn't do anything to hurt me. Without another word, I grabbed the straw from him, bent down and snorted one of the lines. Immediately I tasted bitterness in the back of my throat, which suddenly went numb. Then the sensation hit me. I felt awesome!

I handed the straw to Jed and told him it was cool. He grabbed the straw and snorted a line, leaving one for my dad, who yelled, "Happy New Year!" Then proceeded to do his own line and without saying anything else walked right out of the room. I yelled, "Thanks dad." As he left.

For the next hour Jed and I cleaned my room from top to bottom. All the while talking about things we'd normally not discuss. Cocaine made us totally different people. My room was like most kids' except for a few pieces of furniture. Jay and I had our own beds. We also had a little couch, coffee table, and a dresser with a stereo on top. There were at least six speakers mounted on the walls along with ten different beer posters that I haggled to get from a liquor store owner down the street at Collin's Liquor store.

After a while, Jed and I started to crave more cocaine. It was strange how quickly it took hold of us. I told Jed I was going to ask my dad for some more coke and I would be right back. I headed down the hallway to dad's room. As I walked I could hear Jed singing, "Run to The Hills" by Iron Maiden. He could not sing worth a shit. I almost turned back to tell him to shut his face, but I knew he was high, so I kept going.

Our house had four bedrooms. Jay and I shared one at the end of the hallway. Joey's room was directly across from ours. Halfway down the hall is the bathroom, then two more rooms. The master bedroom where dad and Pauline slept was directly across from Pauline's son David's bedroom.

As I approached dad's room, I could hear Pauline and dad arguing, which was nothing out of the ordinary in those days. Pauline was always drunk since losing her job. I thought it probably wasn't a good idea to ask what I came for, but figured it was New Year's Eve after all, so I knocked.

"What!" Pauline yelled.

"Dad, can I talk to you for a second?"

"No, he's busy!" Pauline replied.

Then I heard dad yelling at Pauline, telling her not to yell at me like that as he opened the door. "What's up son?" He asked.

"Do you have a little more of that coke?"

My dad looked back at Pauline in serious thought, like he wasn't sure. Then he told me to come back in a few minutes. I told him, "Okay." I headed to the kitchen to grab something to drink. My mouth tasted like a dirty ashtray from all the cigarettes we'd been puffing on.

When I opened the refrigerator, all I could see was beer. The house always had plenty of beer in those days. I grabbed a glass, filled it with tap water, and took a few swallows while I waited. After a few minutes I headed back to my dad's room.

Dad was already opening the door by the time I arrived back. He held out his hand and gave me a paper bundle, then told me not to bother him for the rest of the night, shutting the door behind him.

Jed was still singing when I walked back into my bedroom, and I held up my hand showing him what I got from my dad.

"Check it out," I said with a huge grin on my face.

"No way, your dad gave you all the coke? He's cool."

"I know. I'm so lucky Jed."

We snorted a few more lines, making New Year's resolutions that we would never keep.

I had turned thirteen a few months before dad introduced Jed and me to the high of cocaine. I was in the seventh grade and already thought using drugs was normal and cool. Not just me but my friends too. My allowance became a line of cocaine, and since Pauline didn't keep up with the housework, I would receive a line of cocaine for doing the dishes too. I even received coke for washing dad's truck. The sad part was that I bragged about all this to anyone who would listen. It didn't take long for my friends and me to figure out Joey was selling drugs out of the house. Strangers were coming and going all hours of the night. I couldn't stay on the phone for five minutes without Joey yelling at me about tying up the phone line.

Joey was actually pretty cool. He owned a junky Nova and Jay and I would argue over who washed it. Who wouldn't want to. He paid us ten bucks, plus we would normally find an empty pack of cigarettes, full of cash. Not a bad payment for washing a car.

One time Jed and I were sitting in the living room watching MTV, stoned out of our minds from smoking weed. When you opened the front door to our house the living room was directly to the right. Joey, like always, was in a hurry and practically came rushing through the front door; stopped, set a bag down, then continued on to his room. The bag he set down was a clear zip-lock baggie full of cash. We looked back and forth at each other in shock. There was a lot of money in that bag. Before we could say anything else Joey was back to retrieve his bag.

"Hey kids" With a big grin on his face turning back the way he just came from.

Me and all my friends were always in trouble back then. Before school we would stop at Wayne's Liquor Store in Villa Park, smoke some cigarettes and a joint, then race to school. I didn't do any work while I was at school. I couldn't sit still in class. I was far too hyper. My legs wouldn't stop moving, and I just didn't care. I would always ask to go to the bathroom. I didn't really have to go, I just wanted to have a smoke, stretch my legs, then maybe I would return to class. My behavior was bad enough that pretty much all of my teachers hated me. The way I looked didn't help matters. I had long hair and my favorite T-shirt was Ozzy for president. Ozzy Osbourne in the early 80s was really frowned upon. I couldn't compete with all the other kids at my new Junior High School, Cerro Villa. We were considered 'Baggers'. Baggers wore holey jeans, flannel shirts, and had long hair. I hated being called that. Nobody would say it to our faces, but I am fairly certain they wanted to.

I was a bit of a jerk back then and I'm not sure why I acted like that, but I was always mean to the other kids. I was in so much trouble that I earned a Saturday work study for four months straight. For every referral, I received a swat and a Saturday work study. I couldn't believe my dad let that principal give me swats. It only made me rebel more.

Those swats hurt like hell. The paddle was two feet long with holes drilled through it. I would have to place my hands on the back of a chair and "Whack!" Every time Principal Rubin hit me, I wanted to turn around and punch him in the face. That jerk enjoyed it too.

After a night of drinking beers till two in the morning, I had to wake up early for my regularly scheduled "Saturday Work Study." The morning was starting off pretty rough, to say the least. My alarm went off after only 3 ½ hours of sleep, beeping as loud as hell. I knew if I didn't get my ass up I would fall right back to sleep. I put my feet on the floor and stood up. Then I reached over, grabbed a smoke, lit it and headed for the shower. I pulled the shower curtain aside, turned on the hot water, then sat on the toilet to finish my smoke. The next thing I knew I was falling head first into the tub, which caused me to wake instantly. It also severely startled me to the point of a heart attack.

I cleaned up quickly and as I stepped out of the shower I discovered a minor disaster in the bathroom. The countertop was totally filthy. Despite that, I grabbed my toothbrush, rinsed it off, then brushed the remnants of 20 cigarettes and lord knows how many beers out of my mouth, which tasted like an ashtray. Having completed removing the awful taste from my mouth, I left the bathroom.

On the way back to my room I stopped in front of Joey's room noticing that the door was open, which was not normal, especially since Joey was not in his room at that moment. I continued heading back down the hall to the dining room where I found Joey passed out in the chair at the dining room table. I had just found a great way to make my detention much more enjoyable.

I returned to Joey's room, which always seemed very mysterious. Anytime he was coming out of his room he made it a point not to let me and my brother see what was inside. It wasn't easy since our bedroom was right across the hall, but somehow it was managed. Knowing he was asleep in the dining room I stepped inside his bedroom and felt like I had just stepped into another country. The only furniture was a queen size bed, a desk, and a presidential-looking chair that looked really comfortable. There were stained yellow walls from nicotine smoke and no light entered from the window, because Joey had hung a rug over it that blocked out all the light.

There were clothes strewn over the entire floor, and on the desk was a box of sandwich bags, a triple beam scale (to weigh out drugs), a huge bag of cocaine, wads of cash in bags, bags of weed and a very excited thirteen-year-old kid. I grabbed several spoonfuls of cocaine, some weed, two twenty-dollar bills and headed back to my room to finish getting ready for detention. In my room I grabbed everything I would need for the day and headed for the front door.

The Santa Ana winds had dust blowing everywhere, and I could feel the warmth of them brushing my face. I was glad I wouldn't freeze on the way to detention. I retrieved my bike from the side of the house and was on my way to Jed's. It only took me a couple of minutes to arrive and found him waiting out front yelling as I approached, "You're late Homer!"

That was Jed's favorite saying.

"So what dummy. Look what I got!" I replied.

I set my bike down, reached inside my pocket and extracted a bag of my ill-gotten prizes.

"No way! How'd you get all that Chris?" Jed exclaimed excitedly.

"Joey fell asleep in the dining room and left his bedroom door open so I just sort of went in."

"No way. You went inside of Joey's room?"

"Yep. Come on, we've gotta hurry. Will is waiting for us."

On the way to Will's place it felt like we were peddling up a big hill because of the wind. My legs were on fire from having to peddle so hard. Will was waiting out front smoking a cigarette.

"Can you two ever be on time, maybe just once?" Will casually asked.

"Don't blame me, I'm always waiting on Chris." Jed explained.

"Whatever, we're late so we better hurry," I told them both.

The ride to school wasn't any easier with the wind. We peddled with everything we had. By the time we made it to school we barely had time to lock up our bikes. The parking lot was empty, and there wasn't a soul in sight. We ran to Mr.

Spencer's classroom where our day's detention was to take place.

Mr. Spencer was the science teacher, so the class was not set up like a normal classroom. Instead there were a number of tables that seated ten kids each. As we entered we saw Mr. Spencer sitting at his desk with a hot cup of coffee in his hand. He actually looked no better than I felt. I noticed he had a big coffee stain on his shirt as I walked to my desk.

"Gentlemen, find a seat. This can be a very simple day. The rules are easy to understand and follow. There is absolutely no talking and if I catch you talking or playing around, I will dismiss you early, which will mean on Monday morning you will be suspended. Any questions?"

No one said a word. Mr. Spencer picked up a newspaper and sat down at his desk to read it.

There were ten kids in this particular detention and it didn't take long for us to get in trouble. "Why do you guys smell like cigarettes?" One kid asked us.

I looked at Jed, then back at the kid who asked and said, "Why don't you shut up!"

The reaction from Mr. Spencer was an immediate shout, "Curtis! You're out of here and take your friends with you."

"Nice going Curtis," Will added.

"Shut up Will. Chris didn't even do anything." Jed interjected.

We all left the classroom frustrated. These teachers always picked on us and of course we deserved it. Not this time however. Either way I didn't really care and thought the whole incident was funny.

On the way to retrieve our bikes, we got an idea. We decided to break into the school cafeteria. We just had to figure out a way to get inside. On the outside of the cafeteria window was a mesh cage with a tray slot where they handed food out. I thought I could probably fit through if I tried.

"Maybe we should break the window out; that way I might be able to fit through the tray slot." I mentioned to the guys.

Jed walked up, put his foot on the slot and with a couple of kicks, broke the window out, which fell with a crash to the cafeteria floor inside.

"There you go Chris." Jed announced.

I was through in a minute, standing on the cafeteria floor covered in freshly broken glass.

"Meet me at the gym door." I told them and then left.

It felt strange being in there all alone. The cafeteria was connected to the dining hall and the dining hall was connected to the gym. It's in a big building. The further I made my way inside, the darker it became. All those horror movies I'd seen started playing inside my head, which made me more than a little nervous. I felt like Jason Voorhees from "Friday the Thirteenth" was waiting for me just around the corner in the darkness.

When I opened the gym door, it was pitch black. The only light I could see was the two exit signs lit up on the other side of the building. I ran for the closest one. It seemed to take forever to get to that door, and every step reverberated with a loud noise that echoed throughout the building. I finally made it to the door and slowly opened it to Jed and Will, arguing about something. I figured I would scare the crap out of both of them. I flung the door open and yelled, "Freeze!" They both screamed like girls, which made me laugh.

"Fuck'en Chris!" Jed hollered at me.

"Get inside Homer. Hurry! Does anyone know where the light is in here?"

Suddenly the lights came on, blinding me in the process. Jed took that moment to put me into a full Nelson lock.

"Get off me you jock!" I yelled at him.

The gym was huge. It had a basketball court, stage and all sorts of other sporting stuff. There was a gigantic glass case filled with trophies. Obviously, the trophies were from former years of glory. On the stage stood an old piano, lonely and worn from years of use. It was surprisingly my first time being inside the gym.

We made our way to the cafeteria to see what we could find to eat. Once I stepped inside and looked around, it reminded me of a fast food place. The countertops were stainless steel and the room contained the usual walk-in freezer, refrigerator, and storage room for the other foodstuff, not needing to be kept cool.

We began searching for goodies. There was a cart that held large flat cookie sheet pans containing a ton of cookies. The storage room had a whole variety of donuts; powdered, chocolate, and my favorite, crumb.

I was in heaven.

Jed came out of the freezer with a cupcake pan full of change. There was about forty dollars in it. We spent roughly two hours going through the place. We smoked a joint, snorted cocaine, and tried to eat junk food. Which didn't work out well after snorting cocaine. Before finally leaving we filled three paper bags full of junk food. We agreed to come back later that night after we got drunk and have some more fun.

On the way out of the gym I jammed a piece of cardboard inside the door jamb to keep it from locking closed. This way we could just enter easily when we returned later tonight.

Jed said, "That's what they get for kicking us out of detention," As we all exited the building. Since we couldn't go home with all the stuff we stole, we rode to Jenny's house. She lived in the same neighborhood as us and Jed was in love with her. She was really beautiful, so it was obvious why Jed was so smitten.

When we arrived at her house she let us in and immediately started asking all sorts of questions about our newly acquired loot. We, of course being boys, naturally began to brag about our exploits of the day. We snorted some more lines of coke and smoked some pot, never realizing what we had actually done.

We rode our bikes back to the cafeteria that night. We were all drunk from the beer we'd consumed throughout the day. We went back into the building where I had jammed the door and proceeded to completely destroy the place. I broke the trophies in the case removing the remnants of the glories won. The old piano on the stage soon joined the growing pile of broken objects belonging to the school as it crashed into the gym floor from atop the stage. The rest of the evening was spent continuing the destruction of whatever we could get our hands on. When we finally decided to leave, the entire place looked like it had been hit by a Class 5 tornado.

On Monday morning, as we rode up to the bike racks, it was impossible to miss the police presence and investigation units parked in front of the school. We locked up our bikes and casually headed to our lockers. Will was worried we might get busted, as he put it, but I just assured him that as long as we all kept quiet, we'd be alright. Jed gave me an all-knowing look like he knew better, and that what we were in for was not good. He was right. We were called into the office just before lunch and promptly arrested. We were taken to Juvenile Hall, where we spent the night. They released us to our parents the next morning only after promising not to continue getting into trouble.

I was kicked out of that school because they thought I was the problem and simply wanted me out. Jed and Will were allowed to stay at Cerro Villa.

On the way home from Juvenile Hall, my dad was visibly upset with me and wasted no time laying into me.

"Son, what would've happened if the cops came to the house? You could've gotten us all in trouble! Use your head and think about someone other than yourself for a change."

I looked at dad for a second and simply replied, "Alright dad, sorry."

# CHAPTER 4

Trying to tell specific stories about living on Sacramento Street is difficult because most of the time, I was high on drugs. Some incidents still haunt me; living in a drug-infested house drastically changed my life. I smoked a pack of cigarettes a day and marijuana at least twice a day. I snorted cocaine whenever I could get my hands on it too. The worst part was I thought being a drug addict was cool. I was addicted to hard drugs before my fourteenth birthday.

A few months before Pauline moved in with my dad, she had quit her job and took over the dining room table with her Seagram's 7, cigarettes and her authority over us as "Step Mom" made her a force to be reckoned with. When she mixed her drinks with cocaine, her temper was even more hateful. I could do nothing right in her eyes.

One night Pauline sat at the dining room table drunk as usual on Seagram's 7, and high on cocaine. She had a glass jar next to her that contained what looked like a garden slug floating in water. I could hear dad and Joey having a serious argument in the background, so I headed off to the living room to watch MTV. While watching the music videos I overheard a little of what dad and Joey were arguing about. I caught the word "miscarriage," realized what was in the jar and felt sick to my stomach. It was the remnants of a human fetus, the very one she miscarried!

Since my father had gotten a vasectomy years before, it wasn't difficult to figure out what the argument was really about. Pauline never left the house, so there was only one person who could've gotten her pregnant, Joey.

I sat quietly in the living room with a smile on my face smoking my cigarette. Dad would certainly kick Pauline out, and Joey would get the boot too. Surprisingly neither moved out. Over the next several days though, I felt really bad for my dad because his girlfriend and his best friend had slept together. It was beyond my comprehension how he could just go to work every day knowing all the while it was possible they might sleep together again.

One night as I walked through the dining room on my way to the kitchen, I was surprised when a drinking glass flew through the air nearly hitting me in the head. I was able to duck the flying glass, and I just kept on my path to the refrigerator because I was hungry. Apparently Pauline was aiming at my dad but missed and almost got me instead. Fights between them became a recurring event.

Pauline yelled at me, "Chris, get out of the refrigerator!"

"But I'm hungry," I replied.

"Pauline shut up and leave Chris alone." My dad commanded in a menacing tone which kind of shocked me because dad usually sided with Pauline. He then ordered me to go outside and wait in the truck so he could take me to Mcdonald's.

As I walked away towards the front door, I could hear chairs being knocked around and their voices getting even louder as I got to the driveway.

I heard my dad yell at Pauline, "You fucking bitch!" Then I could clearly hear that they were in a scuffle. I went back into the house to see what was going on. Much to my surprise, dad had Pauline pinned to the ground. I noticed a bloody knife lying on the floor nearby. Chairs were overturned and strewn about the room and a picture frame that used to hang on the wall had been knocked down. My dad's leg was covered in blood and he was definitely showing pain on his face from the wound she had inflicted. I could hear Bob Dylan playing on the record player in the background, which felt completely out of place considering the scene before me.

Dad finally let Pauline up, grabbed the knife and limped towards me. He ordered me to "Get in the truck son!" And I turned toward the door but I wanted to know why my dad allowed her to hurt him. I turned to him and simply asked, "Why didn't you just kick her ass dad?"

Dad simply said, "Can't. I'll end up in jail."

Pauline came running out into the front yard ahead of us. Dad just shook his head knowing she wasn't finished fighting yet, and it was clear he was starting to get mad by the look in his eyes. It was then I noticed how badly he was injured. The wound on his leg was just above the knee where she had stabbed him and he was in pain.

Dad and I continued walking toward the front door. We traveled maybe ten more feet when Pauline turned, ran back into the house then came out holding a two-by-four. She looked insane.

"Wayne, if you try and leave I'll throw this piece of wood through your truck window!" She yelled.

Dad quietly said to her, "Pauline, please stop."

I could tell how exhausted he was as he spoke to her. Dad just wanted this nonsense to stop. So did I because my stomach was growling from lack of food.

Pauline looked at him to ensure dad could see what she intended to do. I remember a crazy look on her face, much more menacing because of her bloodshot eyes. Likely her actions were influenced by the drinking and drugs earlier.

"Fuck you Wayne!" She screamed.

As soon as the words flew from her mouth, she flung the board into the air and it slammed directly into the windshield of dad's truck. Anger washed over dad's face and I knew if I didn't do something, he would and I couldn't let that happen. I ran up to Pauline and punched her directly in the face with all my might. I actually enjoyed it.

She stood there completely shocked for a moment, then snapped out of it. She turned and ran back into the house, slamming the door behind her. Dad stood there for a second before limping over to the truck and climbing inside where he sat holding a shirt over his wound and in deep thought. Although I was afraid, I just had to ask, "Dad, what were you two fighting about?"

"I wouldn't give her more cocaine." He answered distantly as if I didn't say anything. In my mind it seemed likely he just didn't want to talk about it anymore, and this probably wasn't a conversation he needed to be having with his fourteen-year-old son.

"Dad, could we please go get something to eat?"

"Hold on son. I have to go check something." Dad responded with suspicion.

He got out and proceeded back into the house and I followed him. The dining room was a disaster. Chairs were lying on their sides and there were broken shards of glass strewn from the living room carpet all the way to the kitchen floor. I couldn't have cared less; I just wanted to eat. Remnants of the fight were scattered along my path as I made my way back to the bedroom. I began thinking, What if she tried to stab me while I was sleeping? I shut my bedroom door behind me and pulled the dresser to block it off and lit a smoke. Throughout the night, I kept waking up from the weird dreams I had.

I attributed them to dad getting stabbed. The dreams were especially bad when she was drinking and doing cocaine, which was 99 percent of the time she was breathing.

Jay ran away soon after all this craziness began. I figured he just couldn't take it anymore. Who could blame him though, right? He ended up in Texas. One day I returned home from school and Jay was gone. At the time I didn't really care because truthfully, we were always fighting anyway. I guess Jay, being a couple of years older, it was easier for him to leave.

Because I was on probation from the destruction at the high school, I was required to see my probation officer at least once a month. Dad would have to come home early from work to drive me to the Probation Department Building, and I of course would get an ear full every time. I didn't mind going because dad would line me up some cocaine. He carried around this little bottle he called a 'Straight Shooter.' It was about half the size of a ChapStick container but about the same thickness. The way it worked was you turn it upside down, tap it on a hard surface, turn a little knob on the side, put it up to your nostril and sniff in the coke. A good line of coke would shoot directly into your nose this way. It was a strange experience watching dad use this little vial. He'd look around cautiously while driving through traffic, tap it on the steering wheel a couple times, check the traffic one more time then take what's called a bump. Then it would be my turn to get a little bump to get ready for my visit with my probation officer.

Most of the visits with that probation officer are vague at best, but I do remember how dad would act with normal adults around. It always seemed a bit phony on those occasions. As of matter of fact that seemed to be his pattern anytime we went to an appointment together.

The Christmas after dad started Jed and me on cocaine was great. I received a carton of smokes, half gram of coke, and a fifty-dollar bill. I was happy as could be at the time. Dad would walk around the house with a big bag of coke singing, "I'm dreaming of a white Christmas." That pretty much ruined that song for me forever. Every time I hear that song, to this day, I am reminded of dad holding a big bag of cocaine. Not a good memory to say the least.

Eventually my mom got wind that I was using cocaine. The rumors had originated out of Marty's bar. Dad had met Joey at the bar, and people that were frequenting the house to buy cocaine knew me. It was inevitable for mom to find out that I was snorting.

Mom decided to rent us a house in Anaheim Hills a few miles from Vista Del Rio Junior High School. There were three acres of land with a pond in the front yard that had some crazy swan and a few ducks.

A few weeks after I left dad's house, the Orange County Drug Task Force raided it. That was the end of residency for my dad and the others on Sacramento Street. I had lived there for almost three years, and my life was changed forever.

Dad bailed out of jail and moved to Silverado Canyon with Pauline. They moved right next door to Pauline's sister. Dad was placed on probation and had to serve ten weekends in the county jail. Joey was sent to prison.

After this when I went to visit my dad, things seemed really strange between us. Pauline acted all nice as if nothing had happened, which irritated me. The facade she put up was obvious and didn't engender trust between us.

Once when I was there Dad called from his room to come to him. With a cigarette in my mouth I headed for his room; memories swam in my head of all the other times he called me to his room over on Sacramento Street to offer me a line of coke. Some things just don't change and this was definitely one of them. As I entered the room dad had a line of coke prepared on the mirror, which I was more than happy to snort up. When I was snorting the thought of Pauline telling me that they had changed rolled around in my brain, and it really irked me how fake that sounded now that I was getting high again. I thanked dad who acknowledged my gratitude.

By the time the sun went down Pauline was drunk and giving me that same old evil look. I just wanted to leave at this point. However, that didn't happen. The next morning, she came in and woke me. She'd made breakfast, so I got out of bed and went to use the bathroom. On the way I had to pass the kitchen. She asked me if I was hungry when I passed by. I thought to myself, *I sure don't miss those mood swings of hers.* I told her I was hungry but to give me a second to wash up first.

I walked into the bathroom and shut the door behind me. I washed up and lit a smoke just to waste time so I didn't have to be alone in the kitchen with Pauline any longer than necessary. The smell of bacon being fried in the kitchen made me hungry.

"Wayne!" Pauline yelled from the kitchen, "Breakfast is ready."

I dropped the cigarette in the toilet and headed toward the kitchen. Pauline asked if I slept alright and if I liked it out here. I said it was a little too quiet for my liking, at which point my dad came in and said, "Good morning."

Pauline then said the craziest thing, "Why don't you come out here and live with us?"

I couldn't believe the crap I was hearing. I simply said, "I don't know, but I'll think about it."

"You'll like it out here," Dad said.

I stood up to go outside and have a cigarette, deliberately avoiding any further discussion. If nothing was said for the rest of my visit, it would suit me just fine. The mere fact that they brought up the subject was shocking to me. It was like my dad was brainwashed or something and Pauline treating me like crap didn't inspire confidence that things would be any better than before.

Not long after I stayed the night at dad's house, mom once again lost the rental house. Dad, true to form, refused to pay child support and mom, ever pride-filled, refused to get public assistance/welfare. Fortunately Jay had come back from Texas and could help financially so we were able to rent a small apartment off Katella Avenue back in the City of Orange. I was glad to be back in Orange once again.

I talked mom into letting me attend Richland Continuation School, the last stop before being placed on Independent Studies. I'd wanted to attend Richland for years because you're allowed to smoke on campus, plus Brian attended the same school. Even though I hated school, I didn't mind going to this particular one all that much. My teacher Mrs. B. was really nice to me, which was a major difference. I was used to teachers hating me. At least that was my perception. Mrs. B., being nice to me, motivated me to try a little harder to do well.

Mom had a new guy named Bill. I instantly disliked him. He didn't have a job and just sat around smoking weed while my mom and Jay were off working to keep a roof over our heads. It bothered me that he didn't even try and contribute.

The apartment on Katella turned into a party house. With Jay paying half the rent, he had more influence on what went on in the apartment. The two-bedroom apartment had five people living there. Mom and Bill took the master bedroom, Jay and his girlfriend Theresa took the other bedroom, which left me a spot on the couch.

Theresa had moved from Idaho to California. She was a runaway. Somehow she had met Jay and they hit it off. Theresa was good looking with blonde hair. So you couldn't really blame him.

Jay's friends had become my friends because I simply drifted apart from all the friends I grew up with. I couldn't stop using drugs and they weren't really into that scene. Plus, after dad's was raided, I ended up living too far away to stay in any friendships.

I had one friend Pat who lived two houses down on Sacramento Street from dad's house. Pat was a good kid. Raised in a Catholic family and attended Catholic school. Until my dad moved into the neighborhood. It wasn't long after he met Jay and me that he was smoking marijuana and doing cocaine, like the rest of us.

Christian was Jay's friend I started hanging around with. Over the years Christian became like an older brother to me. Loved by everyone, and for the next couple of years we spent a lot of time together.

When living with dad he had the ability to scare me, which effectively kept me in line. But living with mom, I did whatever I wanted. I was excited to be living with mom again.

My life involved going to Regal Lanes Bowling Alley, causing trouble in school, and getting high. For the next six months living on Katella Ave., we did as much cocaine as we did living with dad.

It always started out drinking beer with Pat and Christian. By the time we were drunk, Pat had already called his drug connection, and as soon as we received the okay, we were on our way to Santa Ana to score some cocaine.

Santa Ana is a drug infested area in Orange County. Every block has its own gang or two. If you have money or a gun, you can always get drugs in Santa Ana.

I had been following Pat everywhere. Even when I lived on Sacramento St. I would go visit him so I could eat. His house always had food and I was always hungry.

Whenever Pat went to score cocaine in Santa Ana, I usually went along. We'd score and then race back to mom's and party until the sun came up. Partying at home became the norm for us. I never had to go far for drugs unless I wanted to. When I wasn't snorting cocaine, I was smoking weed or drinking.

Once again mom was evicted, pretty much the same as all the other places before now. With no child support and Bill leaching off mom, the rent just didn't get paid. I was fed up with moving back and forth. And I couldn't stand living with Pauline.

It didn't matter how much I begged and pleaded not to be forced to live with my dad. I still ended up there. Mom's not being able to keep up with the bills and rent didn't help matters.

I was now sixteen and living with dad. I had my own network of drug connections. Dad didn't always know where to score, which meant he became reliant on me to score his cocaine. That was okay because scoring coke for dad meant I would get my cut for doing the deed.

Nothing ever changed between Pauline and me. "You're a little punk!" She'd say when she was drunk, which was always. I never did anything right except scoring cocaine for her and dad.

As life continued, I began to set some goals for myself. I decided that once I turned eighteen, I would find a job and give up using drugs. I knew I couldn't go on like this forever. That's all I thought about. And I kept telling myself that I could stop using drugs anytime I wanted.

When I just wanted to go out and drink beers with Christian instead of using cocaine, things would never seem to work out that way. I'd end up having to score coke for dad one way or another. Every Friday I would receive my weekly allowance so I would have to wait for my dad to get home to get paid. Christian would travel down from his dad's house in Riverside, to get to my house to meet with Pat and me. And every week, we'd have to wait on my dad. It was always the same. Dad would see Christian's car in the cul-de-sac and then I would have to go on another cocaine run for him. I didn't mind. Sometimes I had nothing else to do. In fact, I was more than willing because I would get my issue. So I would follow dad into the pad all the while knowing what was about to come.

I'd ask dad for my allowance and explain that Christian and Pat were waiting for me. He'd reach into his pocket and hand me my five dollars. Then he asked if I would go score him some coke before going out with my friends. I just looked at him knowing what was to come. The guilt trip. This one time I wasn't going for it. "Dad, I don't have time. They're waiting for me." And I took off down the stairs.

I wasn't halfway down the stairs before he yelled at me. "Chris, get your ass back in here! You're on restriction for not taking out the trash. Tell your friends you can't go, then take out the trash and go to your room."

So, I went out to the car and explained what had just happened to my friends, who like me, thought it was a stupid reason to be placed on restriction, but understood. They said they would call later to see if maybe he'd let me off early, and I agreed and said goodbye.

Bummed out I made my way back into the apartment to take out the trash, which was only a quarter of the way full. This made me pretty angry as I pulled the bag out of the can. I took it to the dumpster and then went straight to my room.

Dad came to my room about five minutes later to find me staring up at my ceiling fan and asked me to score him some cocaine. Of course, now I didn't have much of a choice. It was either score pop some coke or be stuck all Friday night in my room. Only problem now was finding a ride to Santa Ana. Without Pat or Christian to give me a ride, things would be more complicated. I would have to ride to Dee's house in Villa Park, then have him take me to Santa Ana. Which was no picnic. With every block having its own gang, staying out of trouble was not always easy. Dad telling me to stay out of trouble seemed ironic and confusing. Since sending me into a "Hot Spot" like Santa Ana to score him coke was the opposite of staying out of trouble. Most times I was been lucky not to be robbed or shot.

People who often went there were pulled over by the local police and busted for what was going on there. I always wondered what my dad would do if I were to get busted scoring him cocaine. It didn't seem to stop him from asking. Already having a record for being busted in the school cafeteria incident didn't make me feel any less easy about the task at hand.

I returned safely and received a line for my efforts and an extra five bucks. I guess as a bonus. He explained that I would be receiving a break this time, and I was free man, off restriction. But not before reminding me not to neglect my chores ever again. I was totally happy about the trade-off at the time.

Realizing what happened on that particular Friday night with him placing me on restriction with virtually no reason took me years to grasp. When I finally did realize why he put me on restriction (for not scoring him cocaine) it caused me deep-seated anger towards him and Pauline.

# CHAPTER 5

Everything seemed to be falling apart, not that it was ever any good before, but things certainly were not improving with time. I became more and more detached and not able to deal with the abuse inflicted on me, even though at that time I couldn't understand it. When dad first gave me cocaine, I thought he was the best dad in the world. However, when I was punished into scoring cocaine for him regularly, it made me feel like it was the only reason he wanted me around. Once I made the connection and realized the truth, it hit me hard and I instantly began to rebel.

One day I stopped coming home. Instead, I stayed at my brother's apartment. Jay and Theresa had rented a place a few miles away from where dad lived. We did cocaine day and night. It was the only steady thing in my life, which made me feel no pain.

I began cashing stolen checks so we could all get high, and school pretty much ended for me there too. It didn't take Jay long to lose the apartment since he had no job. None of the bills were paid so consequently we ended up moving in with my mom and her worthless boyfriend. Mom had landed a job at the Penny Saver off State College and La Palma, in the city of Anaheim. Mom was actually happy to be supporting herself.

Anaheim was a major change for me. Mom rented an apartment near known gangs. La Jolla was the most known gang in that area. The apartment was located on Parkland. This was totally different from the city of Orange. Mexicans were the majority of tenants in the area. I actually enjoyed the excitement that came with my new home.

I was selling cocaine and making runs back and forth to Santa Ana at all hours of the night. I would steal mom's boyfriend's junky ass car and race to Santa Ana to score. He never found out, either. I became well known with all the drug connections in that area. The gang known as "Loper's" ran that whole area. I was only a teenager and as far as I could see the only whiteboy who showed up to buy drugs at three in the morning.

After a few months of living with mom, police investigators for the Orange Police Department started calling the apartment. They were investigating all those stolen checks I was cashing while living with my brother.

I was in our alleyway one day smoking some cocaine which was how I spent most of my time lately. I looked up and saw mom approaching. She had a worried look on her face.

"Chris, we have to talk to that police investigator about those checks you cashed."

I looked up from the desk I had set up and asked, "Will I be going to Juvenile Hall?"

She replied, "No, Chris. They just want to speak with you."

I agreed to do as she asked, and she informed me that it was to take place Tuesday, and to make sure I was around. I told her I would and asked to be alone.

Despite the looming investigation, I continued right on with my little drug spree, which included stealing and selling cocaine in order to stay high. My life was a complete disaster. Cocaine had sucked the life out of me.

Tuesday arrived in no time at all. The night before mom

made sure I was at home. On that morning we drove to the City of Orange Police Department, and it just happened to be the same location as when I had to report to the probation officer. However, this time there was no cocaine to be shared as I was with mom.

I'd felt very uneasy about the police placing me back into Juvenile Hall. The whole thing about talking to the investigator wasn't sitting well with me. Mom assured me that I wouldn't be arrested, and I believed her because she would never lie to me like that.

We listened to music on the drive all the way to Orange, and I smoked cigarettes to calm my nerves welling inside. We pulled into the parking lot at the police station and set off to the entrance.

"Chris, how do you know where we're going?" Mom asked.

"Dad had to bring me here to visit my probation officer."

"Oh yeah I remember that." She replied.

I opened the entrance door holding it open for my mom, then followed her inside. The investigator was waiting for us. He greeted my mom formally and asked us to follow him.

The police department was well lit and filled with people. There were desks littered with paperwork. We followed the investigator down a hall into his office and sat in the chairs in front of his desk.

Things didn't feel so bad I said to myself. I couldn't have been more wrong. Another investigator walked in at that moment and asked me to stand up. I stood up and asked what was going on. To my surprise, I was placed in handcuffs and promptly arrested for fraud.

"Son of a bitch! Really mom? How could you lie to me like that?"

"I'm really sorry Chris." She whispered as tears filled her eyes. "You need help that I can't give you. I'm sorry honey, but it's for your own good."

I was escorted by an investigator down a long hall and placed in a holding cell. I couldn't believe my own mom had set me up, and it made me even angrier. I couldn't believe this was happening to me.

There was no getting out of Juvenile Hall this time, and I spent the next 60 days out of a 90-day sentence locked up. It felt like I was never going to be released. Sixty days in the Hall is a lifetime to a kid. The feeling of being sent to Juvenile Hall as a teen was scary as hell.

It is not an experience easily forgotten. Most of the kids were up and coming gang bangers and were better off in the Hall. Several kids from Orange County had been found dead. Death came from gunshot wounds inflicted by rival gangs in Santa Ana, Anaheim, Garden Grove, etc. So being placed in the hall was somewhat of a saving grace for those kids involved with gangs. At least they would live a little while longer in the Hall. It probably saved my life too, because I was using so much cocaine, I was bound to kill myself if I kept on with the way I was going.

Juvenile Hall was an experience I'll never forget. I remember how the shampoo smelled to this day. Even the loud clacking of the cell doors. My first morning at breakfast I felt that the teenagers were all staring at me.

Maybe because I was the only white kid, and I am certain I was the smallest kid. The thought of me making it through this place was not going well inside my head.

After a few weeks I felt a lot easier about my situation in the Hall. The "Hall" is what all the kid's called Juvenile Hall. In no time at all I was playing sports, working out, and acting tough, and surviving like the rest of the teenagers. Sixty days flew by, it seemed. I spent the next 30 days in The Care Unit, which is a rehab center for people with a variety of problems like drugs, family etc. Care unit was a vacation compared to the Hall. There was a soda machine, snacks, a cafeteria and a nice garden to smoke cigarettes several times a day.

Everyone was encouraged to talk about their deepest secrets and problems. Group meetings were pure torture though. Several times a day these meetings were held along with school, which was mandatory for adolescents.

Within two weeks my mindset had completely changed. I told myself that I would never do drugs again and I was adamant about it. My mom was certainly pleased with my new attitude. I left 30 days later with a much more positive outlook on my life. Too bad I went back to the same environment where my troubles began. It pretty much was a recipe for failure, and ultimately, I fell back into the same pattern.

I was back on probation but this time I had to undergo drug testing once a week on average. Home life at first seemed really good. Bill, my mom's boyfriend, was playing the part, but the situation would change very rapidly. Bill still didn't work and smoked weed all day in the apartment. This was not conducive to my recovery. I shouldn't have been exposed to that kind of environment so soon after getting out of rehab. I told myself that it would not be a problem, but what did I know?

A few weeks after I arrived back home Bill told me that smoking weed was okay and that I wouldn't be tested for it. I was 16 years old and naive so I started smoking weed with him, thinking it would be a good idea. Fortunately, I actually didn't get tested for weed. It didn't take long for me to smoke weed every day. I mean, I was great at ruining my life.

Anaheim was so different than living in the City of Orange. Walking down the street was dangerous. You could be caught in the wrong place at the wrong time and be hurt or even killed. The gangs in the surrounding areas did not forgive anyone. I'd hear gunshots at night all the time and even in the daytime. I made it a point not to be running around in the alleyways at night by myself, just to be on the safe side.

I met Tommy about a month after being released from the Hall. He lived next door to us and it wasn't long before I started hanging out at his place. Tommy was older and out of school so whenever I'd get into arguments with Bill, which was pretty frequent, I would go to Tommy's place. Tommy was a mellow guy. He liked to smoke weed and we listened to the same music. I felt comfortable around him, which was unusual those days for me. Tommy accepted me the way I was.

I discovered that Tommy used a lot of meth. I didn't get involved at first, but after hanging around, I was bound to experiment with the drug. I mean, why not? Tommy had a job and seemed to be doing well while using meth. So why couldn't I?

Wow! meth was totally different than using cocaine. Instead of locking myself away in a room, I was out and about constantly on the move. I thought to myself that using cocaine for so long was nowhere near as good as meth because with coke I would only be high for a short time, as with meth I would stay high for hours on end.

Meth made me feel alive like never before. It wasn't too long before I was hooked on meth. Two months later, I gave a positive urinalysis for meth.

I had simply traded one addiction for another. My probation officer put me on house arrest until my court date. This was much better than going straight to the Hall. Now I could sit at home all day and smoke weed and hang out with my friends. I wasn't really supposed to have friends over but we found a way to make it work.

My buddy would park in front of the apartment and I would sit on the grass. We'd smoke weed and shoot the shit. One time my probation officer pulled up as soon as we finished smoking a joint. My buddy just drove off without a word and looking back on it now makes me laugh.

I went to court a few weeks later and was sentenced to 60 more days in YGC (Youth Guidance Center). Once I finished my time there, I went back to live with my dad in Laguna Niguel. I didn't stay long even though it was a pretty nice place to live.

Living with them was weird because I wasn't allowed in the apartment unless dad or Pauline were home, this created a unique situation for me, and not in a really good way.

My brother was scoring cocaine for them now, which made me obsolete. They had sworn to me that they were no longer using drugs, another lie in the very long list of lies. Because of their influence I had grown up high all the time.

Dad may have kept a roof over my head but you could make the argument that there was never any real parenting happening and consequently, I was a mess, and soon I would be 18 years old. I was counting the days because I would receive a cash settlement on my 18th birthday.

Christian, me and a few others were sideswiped by some lady in a Ford Pinto when we were making a left hand turn at an intersection. Out of nowhere SMASH! We were hit and I ended up in the hospital. Christian broke his arm. I almost lost my arm after my finger got infected and I ended up in the hospital. This resulted in me receiving a settlement once I turned 18. I was excited and couldn't wait to buy a car, then start my life.

On my 18th birthday, I immediately returned to Anaheim to talk to my mom, who had been dodging me. I set my mind to have a talk with her. It wasn't a week after having to return from Laguna Niguel that I received a call from the bank where my settlement deposit had been placed for me.

Turns out my mom had withdrawn the money illegally and I was screwed. I was very upset! It was inconceivable to me that she could do this. It wouldn't have bothered me so much had she at least spent the money on herself, but knowing that her boyfriend had probably helped her spend the money really pissed me off. I fantasized about draggin' his ass behind a car all over Anaheim. I hated him using my mom like that and treating her like shit on top of that, which only made me hate him more.

I made my mom buy me some transportation so I could find a job. She bought me a Yamaha scooter with a top speed of about 60 mph, and I absolutely loved the freedom it gave me. Being mobile for the first time in my life is something I'll always remember.

I moved back in with my mom, and for a time that made me very happy. I landed a job at Round Table Pizza in Yorba Linda, and it was a lot of fun to work there.

There was a Marine Recruiting station next to where I worked and I noticed the Marines walking in and out every

47

day. They reminded me of my grandpa serving during WWII. This was definitely something I needed, structure, discipline, and rules to follow. Life thus far had been nothing more than a circus. This could be the solution.

After work one day I strolled into the recruiter's office intending to sign up. The recruiter asked if I had a diploma, which I didn't, and everything went downhill from there. I was pissed off that I couldn't get in. I mean they could draft all those guys to Vietnam who didn't want to go into the service, yet I couldn't volunteer. At that moment, I knew I was headed for a disaster.

A few weeks later I lost my scooter. I was speeding on my way home from work and I had neither a driver's license nor registration when stopped so I lost my transportation. This resulted in me having to give up my job because it was too far away for me to travel. I was back running around the neighborhood.

One day I was returning from the liquor store in my mom's car when I spotted this beautiful girl walking down the street. I took a chance and pulled beside her and asked her if she needed a ride. To my surprise, she smiled and said yes. As she stepped into the car I noticed her blue eyes, and with her long blonde hair, she was irresistible. I was having a hard time finding the right words to say. Tiffany ended up being my first love.

Over time I lost Tiffany because of my drug problem, but I became good friends with Tiffany's best friend, Michele. Michele had a guy she hung out with at the time named Nick. And since we all used a lot of drugs, we became good friends.

Michele was also good looking with her blonde hair. I started running the streets with Nick. We had this little scam to earn money. We'd drive around Anaheim in Nick's Toyota truck searching the neighborhoods for aluminum cans on the sides of houses. We'd spot the plastic bags full of cans as we drove past the houses. We actually got really good at it.

I'd write down the addresses and later that night Nick and I would come back and fill the truck up with the cans. Some nights we would make up to $150. Not a bad night's work for a couple of tweakers.

While searching one night, we were pulled over by a cop. I had a warrant for my arrest for failure to pay fines for driving without a license or insurance on my scooter. This landed me in the Orange County jail for 40 days. My first time in an adult jail.

During that time in jail my family moved to Mission Viejo. After getting released from jail, I bounced around and stayed with friends but ultimately, I ended up in Mission Viejo with my mom.

It wasn't much different than living in Laguna Niguel. Another paradise city full of rich people that I had nothing in common with. I landed a job at a Mobile Gas Station. This was a kickback job. I wasn't on meth because I couldn't find it, not yet anyway. It wasn't long before I met Brad and Andy. They both came from wealthy families.

Brad owned a van that we rode to parties. I ended up driving home most of the time because Brad was too drunk. He'd become so wasted from drinking that we would have to drag him to the van, but you couldn't have asked for a better friend.

Andy was the total opposite of Brad and me. He took college courses and dressed like a jock. At first glance you would think Brad and I had been friends a long time, while Andy looked out of place, not to mention a little strange. He had a weird laugh that drew a lot of attention.

One night after a party we had to drag Brad out to the van once again. Once Andy and I got him in the back, we jumped in and I started to drive. As we were about to pass the 5 freeway I decided to drive to Anaheim.

Andy asked where we were going and I told him Anaheim. "I wanna score some meth."

Andy objected stating Brad didn't want me driving out to Anaheim. I explained to Andy not to worry because Brad was out cold, drunk.

I arrived in Anaheim without incident and Andy

commented that the place looked like a dump, which made me laugh. I parked out in front of Tommy's pad who still lived next door to my mom's old apartment and went in to score a little meth.

Brad was trying to take a piss just outside when I returned and stumbled around while trying to do so.

I convinced him to go in the nearby alley to do his business but forgot to warn him about the local gang bangers who periodically roamed that particular alleyway. When a fair amount of time passed and Brad didn't return, I kind of knew something was wrong. As I thought about it, I said, "Oh Shit!" And ran into the alley to find my friend covered in blood and lying on the ground. I ran back to get Andy to help me drag him back to the van so we could get home. I took Andy home and parked the van in front of my house to let Brad sleep in there, since he was in no condition to drive home.

The next morning, I went out front to wake up Brad. I'd been up all night tweaking in my garage. When I slid open the van's side door, Brad was sitting up smoking a cigarette. He asked me what had happened the night before, even though we both knew he didn't really want the answer considering the dried-up blood on his shirt was evidence something had gone wrong.

I explained what happened. He asked why I drove to Anaheim, and I told him I had asked him and he gave me the okay. He didn't remember doing so, which I laughed at.

Mom ended up losing that house too. Mission Viejo is an expensive place to live, and my aunt just couldn't let us live there for free. I ended up back in Anaheim where I liked it better anyway.

What I didn't know was that moving back to Anaheim would be the biggest mistake of my life. Not just moving back but moving back completely on my own. I either found a job, or I didn't eat or have a place to sleep.

I eventually moved with friends and landed a job with a telemarketing company. After living with friends for a few months, I moved into the Seville Motel. I was about to receive the second part of my settlement. This part was $3,000 but it bought me a 1971 Chevy Nova. My first car making me mobile again.

Living at the Seville Motel wasn't working out well. One night after returning home from dropping this girl off, I was walking up the stairs and cops came out of everywhere with guns drawn and pointed right at me.

"Get on the ground!" The Anaheim police yelled.

I was handcuffed and placed in the back of a waiting police car. They asked me a bunch of questions. Somebody had robbed the front desk and I fit the description. They took me to the Orange County jail. I was released 24 hours later, saying they would be in touch. When I got back to my room at the motel I just packed up and split.

I moved in with this girl named Brenda. She was living with some friends. It was one of those apartments where everybody was brother and sister, and the older lady was the mom. Me, being the only one with a job, didn't get along with anyone. There were all on welfare and this place was a nightmare! To make a long story short, I got into a fight at Brenda's and somehow ended up staying with Suzy for a few nights.

A few weeks after I moved in, I met Brenda's sister Suzy. She was about 24 years old. I had just turned nineteen. Suzy was by far the most beautiful girl I had ever seen. I couldn't stop looking at her. Everything about Suzy was sexy. I was so attracted to her that I couldn't think straight.

Suzy's boyfriend was worthless in my eyes. He wouldn't get a job and it seemed every day that I returned home from work, he was parked on the couch doing nothing and had not even attempted to find a job. His excuse was he was tired of looking and that no one wanted to hire him anyway.

He basically gave up and I decided it was best to help him so I got him a job with me. This turned out not to be a great plan because I shit you not, he stole some girl's wallet on his very first day.

I wasn't a tough guy and decided it was best left alone, but it wasn't long before things began to go seriously wrong, and he had no one to blame but himself in the end.

Suzy's son Brandon and I became close. After work I would take him to the park. We'd run around, acting stupid as kids usually do and play. Suzy started keeping an eye on me. Next thing I knew I kicked the boyfriend out of the apartment and fell in love with Suzy.

Work was going well but the telemarketing company I had been working for was shut down. I showed up one morning for work and no one was there. No one knew what had happened. A coworker asked if I wanted to work for them as they started a new company of their own. I wasn't too sure about the telemarketing business, but it wasn't long before I was making about $2,000 a week. Life was good. We'd been using a lot of meth together and thought "Why not?" The money was flowing pretty nicely, and the bills were caught up so we indulged.

The problems in the weeks to come were not something that I would easily forget. Our apartment was robbed. My brand new stereo system was taken, along with Suzy's new TV, and some other personal items. This whole situation caused a lot of problems in our relationship. After the robbery there was a lot of uncertainty between Suzy and me. The new company was raided by the Feds and shut down.

Some co-workers contacted me and wanted me to go to work for them in Salt Lake City, Utah. It was a new start up company. The telemarking laws in Utah, weren't as harsh as California. Plus the bond to run a 1-5 promotion in Utah was only $500, compared to California's $100,000 cost. At this time I was about 20 years old when I helped start this company.

I'd fly back to John Wayne Airport on Friday, score meth and fly back to Utah on Sunday night, well at least until this one flight home. Turbulence always made me nervous this time flying home the plane was shaking like crazy. This seriously scared me to death, and I promised myself if I ever got back on the ground again I'd never get back into another plane.

I stepped off that plane, grabbed my luggage, walked up to

my boss and told him I would never step on a plane again. He tried talking me into driving up to Utah and staying, but I was too hooked on meth and wanted to stay right where I was. I got out of the telemarketing business.

Plus, the business was becoming too risky. Almost everyone I knew in the telemarketing business that worked in California was being charged with the RICO Act. In the early 90s, telemarketing was big news, and it wasn't good news. When the cops raided the company I had worked for, I was lucky only because I showed up late that day.

Two years later a briefcase recovered from that raid ended up in front of me. I was arrested for cashing stolen checks by the Fullerton PD. when a detective walked in with the briefcase. He asked if the briefcase was mine, and I sat there completely stunned.

People who worked in the telemarketing business were receiving 30-40 year sentences under the Federal RICO Act. Naturally I didn't claim knowledge of the briefcase and went as far as saying I had never seen it, even though there were two tickets for driving without a license in my name inside the briefcase.

# CHAPTER 6

I found myself back on the east side of Anaheim in a neighborhood off Rio Vista and Lincoln. In the early 90s this place was crawling with: tweakers, speed freaks, and crankster gangsters. Whatever name you could put on meth users, they were there.

The only person I really knew was Michele. I was an outsider and didn't fit in. I was living out of my 66 Chevy Van I had recently bought. I was selling meth to stay high and soon found out how tough selling drugs is while living on the streets.

For the next several months I learned how cruel people could actually be. You could not trust anyone even if you knew them. My biggest mistake was thinking people could be trusted. All I wanted to do was sell meth, stay high, and fit in. That was not realistic and didn't end up working out well for me.

I was beat up, bullied, robbed, and generally taken advantage of for months on end. The sad part - I kept coming back for more. I guess because I had no place else to go. My mom could only afford one drug addict which turned out to be her useless ass boyfriend who still had no job, and I could still not understand that fact. It felt like she chose him over me.

All these people on the east side of Anaheim grew up together in one way or another. My only connection was Michele, whom I had met through Tiffany.

Then Dina came into my life. She was a very good looking woman with blondish hair and slim for her height. She was also very tough, which I figured was because she had been to prison for eighteen months. She had a son named Kenny. She completely fascinated me.

When I met Dina, I was beaten down from the streets. So far all the streets had done for me was turn me into a scandalous idiot. I wasn't considered tough by any standard, nor did I aspire to be either.

I started out buying meth from Dina. I'd give her a little money and she would hand me a lot of meth. I would sell a lot, but I'd do a lot too. I would come back the next day with only half the money. She would tell me how much I owed her and then give me more meth.

After about a month of that, I owed her $600 roughly. So, when I walked into her place one day, she just started laughing at me, which puzzled me, of course. I asked her why she was laughing, and she replied, "Because you always come back, and people who owe me as much as you do usually just disappear." I wasn't sure how she meant that, so I just shrugged it off as her sense of humor.

I had made plans to meet with a girl named Katrina, that I met earlier that day while delivering dope. We were going to hook up that night. She was so good looking I could not refuse. I told her I would get ahold of her later after I finished with my errands. I was already late meeting with Dina.

After meeting Dina, I did hook up with Katrina but having had no sleep the night before made me extremely tired. At about 10 PM Katrina and I had been running around together and even though I barely knew her, we decided to rent a motel room. I thought to myself, "What was the worst thing that could happen?"

I told her to drive to the Fairfield Inn located in Placentia because it wasn't somewhere cops usually go to search for something or someone suspicious.

On the way to the hotel, I fell asleep, and Katrina drove to the wrong hotel in Fullerton. Anyone who knew anything about Orange County knew to stay out of Fullerton because the cops are treacherous and if you looked remotely suspicious, you would be harassed by them.

I stepped out of the car and grabbed my duffle bag that contained a sawed-off shotgun. I had gotten it as payment for a debt earlier that day. I didn't want to carry that thing around, but I had been in a hurry. I even gave up the opportunity to sell it to some gang bangers earlier so I ended up lugging it in my duffle bag.

I thought we were in Anaheim when we got inside the room. I pulled out the shotgun and began wiping it down to remove the fingerprints, and when I finished, I leaned it up against the wall. Not more than a couple of minutes later there was a knock at the door. I peeked through the peephole and saw two uniformed officers and thought, "Son of a bitch!"

"Katrina, there are a couple of security guards outside."

She came running to the door and opened it. That was when all hell broke loose.

"KEEP YOUR HANDS WHERE I CAN SEE THEM!" The officer yelled.

I immediately noticed that the two officers were Fullerton Policemen. I backed up and sat on the bed, pulled out half an ounce of dope from my pocket and slid it under the pillow, then got on the floor. I couldn't understand why she opened the door and her doing so gave me no time to think.

When the cops saw the shotgun, we were placed in handcuffs, and not long after, the dope was found too. So off to the cop-shop we were carted.

Once we arrived, I could hear Katrina crying and telling the cops that the stuff belonged to me. She repeated that several times as I sat there in the next holding cell.

My one phone call was to Dina, and I explained everything

to her. What was found by the cops, etc. I also mentioned what Katrina had said to the cops.

"Don't admit to that stuff being yours." Dina had said, "because if you do, you'll be sent to prison. Call me once you get through booking."

I hung up the phone and went back to the holding tank. A little while later the police transported me to the main jail in Orange County, called OCJ. The whole way there the cops are telling me that I am going to prison and I'll be raped and all sorts of crap. I just laughed at them.

Once I made it through booking at OCJ I called Dina. She explained to me that they could only hold me for three days and then they had to let me go. She told me to call her when they released me.

Sure enough I sat in court for three days, they never called me, and I was released at one o'clock in the morning on the third day.

As soon as I stepped through the door of OCJ's parking lot I could smell cigarette smoke. Two girl's, waiting for someone to be released undoubtedly, were sitting by a pay phone, so I bummed a smoke from them. I picked up the phone to call Dina. Surprisingly she answered the phone on the first ring.

"Chris, I had a feeling it would be you. Are you out?"

"Yeah, you were right. How'd you know I'd be out in three days?" I asked.

"Well Chris, I've been around for a while. Stay in front of the jail and I'll send someone to get you."

I told her I would and thanked her. From that day on I placed a lot of trust in Dina. She actually cared about me, and after all the crap I'd been through since I started running the streets, this whole situation was something entirely new to me.

An hour later Flaco drove up with Chico in Dina's lowered truck. Flaco and Chico were from the same gang, and Flaco was seeing Dina. I didn't really know either one. I just knew that they sort of protected her from being robbed. Flaco yelled out the driver's side window, "Hurry up and get in the truck" as he put it, "this place is a bust!" I just laughed, jumped in and we drove off.

On the way to Dina's apartment, I explained the whole story of what had happened in the motel. Flaco said I was lucky I had wiped the fingerprints off the shotgun when I did. I told him I felt bad for Katrina. He told me not to worry about it because it's all part of the game, and she should of kept her mouth shut anyway.

When we made it back to Dina's, I walked upstairs to her room, and as usual she was weighing out dope. She told me it would be a good idea for me to hang around the house for a while. I owed her about $700 dollars.

The pad was actually cool. There were a few girls who hung out, cleaned and watched Little Kenny. I looked at Little Kenny and thought to myself that the kid was pretty much growing up the same way I had.

It didn't take long for me to get bored hanging around the apartment. I had only been out of jail for one day. The apartment was two stories tall with one bedroom and a bathroom upstairs. The living room and kitchen were downstairs. The kitchen had a little dining room with a sliding glass door that led into the alley. The whole block was run down, and it made perfect sense in terms of the meth business. I don't think a night went by without me hearing gunshots in the neighborhood.

One night I was eating in the kitchen when Flaco came through the sliding glass door with Chico. They were both carrying stereo equipment. I asked them where they had gotten the equipment because it wasn't garbage in terms of quality. They both had Alpine stereos, amps, and woofers.

"We went shopping," Chico said.

That was their street slang for stealing car stereos in the middle of the night. I couldn't help but laugh at that comment.

In the following weeks Flaco and I started talking more. We were from completely different backgrounds. He grew up gangbanging and I grew up doing a lot of drugs.

I was smoking meth one night in the living room, bored to death, when Flaco came walking downstairs and told me to come with him. I jumped up immediately and was shocked because I had never gone anywhere with him except when he picked me up from jail. I wondered what was going on but decided that it was better than being stuck in the apartment, bored. I simply asked where we were headed. He told me that we were going shopping.

We drove about fifteen minutes away into a neighborhood I wasn't familiar with and parked. We headed out on foot and began scoping out the cars. I did my best to keep quiet while trailing Flaco and smoking a cigarette. I had no experience doing anything like this. I might have once when I was drunk and too intoxicated to remember.

Flaco didn't take long to locate a car that had a nice stereo. He instructed me to keep watch and let him know if anyone was approaching. The code was to knock on the car to let him know.

It took him about two minutes to get into this Honda Civic. I kept just out of sight in a spot where I could easily observe the street in both directions. I heard Flaco cuss and then mumbled something. He stood up just outside the door of the car and tossed me the keys to Dina's truck telling me to get it and drive back to the apartment. He said he'd meet me there because it was going to take some time to get the car stereo out of this particular car, and doing it there would be too risky so he planned to take the whole car.

I ran back to the truck, jumped in and as soon as I started it, Flaco pulled up beside me and signaled me to follow him, which I did. We parked in an alleyway behind the apartment and he went to work on the stereo.

I observed him as he worked furiously to get the stereo out and asked him why he bothered to steal them when he didn't really need the money in the first place. He simply explained that he needed the extra money. After we finished, we retired back to the apartment and smoked some more meth.

The apartment, in the following weeks, became more and more chaotic. There were fights, arguments, and enough foot traffic that a light should've been installed. My dad's house growing up was bad, but nothing compared to this place. Everyone in this place seemed to carry a gun. Little Kenny went about his young life as if nothing was out of the ordinary.

I thought spending more time with Kenny would be important. One afternoon after we had just returned from McDonalds Dina was waiting with a big smile on her face and said for me to follow her into the alleyway. She had bought something for all of us.

I followed her out the sliding glass door that led out to the alley with Little Kenny following on my heels. Coming into the alley, I saw an old 67 Chevy Van parked. It immediately reminded me of my old Chevy Van, I used to live in.

When I opened the door, I noticed some differences like the gear shifter was on the dashboard, it had more windows, and was a V 8. After inspecting the van, I picked up Little Kenny who was excited, threw him over my shoulder and went back into the apartment.

Dina was eating a bowl of cereal at the table when we entered and asked if I liked the new van. I, of course, told her I was more than happy and told her how it reminded me of my old van and the memories that went with it. She explained I would be using the van to collect money from people who owed her debts. I gratefully agreed and thanked her for her generosity. Without even trying each day I was involving myself more with this clique. I tried to stay away from the pad as much as possible even taking Little Kenny with me to keep him away too and keep him from seeing all the things a child shouldn't be exposed to.

Another guy started hanging around the pad too. His name was Matt. He was in a gang called Crazy White Boys. He was from the Garden Grove area and now it was the four of us. I couldn't always avoid going with them all the time and found myself doing crimes that carry a lot ofprison time. We were all in the van one day on our way to this house. This guy, Mark owed Dina almost $1,000. He wasn't returning her calls. We're all spun out on meth and packing guns. Flaco was telling Matt he hated white people while I'm driving to this house.

We parked in the alley so we could go through the backyard. When we opened the gate I noticed trash, bike parts, and car tires littered all over the backyard. This was a tweaker pad. I counted at least seven people right away. Mark came through the back door and asked what we wanted. Flaco looks around and casually says that Dina wants her money. The reply was that he didn't have any money right now and he had to pay rent and -BAM!

Chico walked straight up to Mark with a mag lite in his hand and cracked him on the side of the head. Mark went straight down to the ground. Mark looked up at Chico, eyes wide open and cried, "Okay! Okay! I have a little money in the house."

"Who else is inside the house?" Matt yelled.

"Just my girlfriend." Mark explained.

"I'm going inside with you to make sure you don't try anything hinky," Mark replied, "Get your stupid ass up."

Hinky means, scandalous you could say. For example, that hinky bum stole my bike.

Matt followed Mark inside while we all stayed in the backyard. Mark's friends looked like they'd seen a ghost. He came out of the house and announced that he got about $500 bucks from Mark.

"Alright Mark, do we have to return, or will you come by with the rest of the cash in a few days?" Flaco asked.

"I'll have in a few days." Mark promised and we left without another word. I had no gun and just quietly watched the thing happen.

When we returned to Dina's we all sat around smokin' speed and laughing about Mark being struck in the head with a mag lite.

Little Kenny came running down the stairs asking if I wanted to go to Mcdonald's. He was jumping all around. I took him upstairs to explain to Dina I was taking him for a few hours. The pad was about to be flooded anyway with people coming over to buy meth.

Later that night when I returned with Little Kenny, I had to carry him inside the apartment. He fell asleep as usual in the car. After I had put him in his bed, I came back downstairs. I was the only one there with long hair and looked harmless compared to the others I was hanging around with. Flaco was sitting in the living room with a few people I had never seen before.

Some guy made some smartass remark as I walked into the kitchen to grab something to drink. I didn't acknowledge the guy. A second later Flaco walks into the kitchen and asks me why I let that guy talk to me like that. I told him I didn't care what that dude said, and immediately Flaco got in my face saying, "You can't let people talk to you like that, Chris. And if I ever find out you let someone disrespect you again, Chico and I are going to beat the shit out of you." I thought to myself, *Whatever,* as he walked away.

The next day I went to Sears with some stolen credit cards. A Homeboy had given them to me. I've used stolen credit cards in the past. I walked straight for the clothes; grabbed new 501 jeans, some white t-shirts, and a few other things I thought I could use. Then I found a cashier so I could pay for them.

I told the lady that I would like to pay with my credit card and handed her the card which she slid through the card reader. She asked me if I could hold on for a second. I of course said sure and two seconds later a man's voice behind me ordered me to place my hands on top of my head.

*Son of a bitch.* I thought to myself. At that moment I knew I was busted. This happened in January of 1994. I was sentenced to 45 days in jail and sent to the "Farm" a branch of the Orange County jail.

I was released 45 days later and went right back to Dina's, and right back using meth again.

Little Kenny asked me how work was because that's what his mom told him because he was too young for the actual truth about my activities.

By this time, we were becoming our own little gang. I wasn't as familiar with the streets as everyone else, but I was learning fast.

Flaco took me with him everywhere. It was impossible for me to avoid it. We'd stop by his parents and eat, and then be off to whatever mission we had planned. I was even dressing like a gangster by this time, baggy pants, and white t-shirts. It wasn't long before running around with a gangbanger almost cost me my life.

One day as we were leaving Flaco's parents' house, Flaco said he wanted to go check out this neighborhood, so we'll have something to do later that night.

As funny as it sounds Flaco refused to go shopping in his own neighborhood. So here we are in the middle of the afternoon in what we later realized was "Traveler's" neighborhood. That was a notorious gang in Anaheim. We walked around looking for targets to come back and hit that night. A car came cruising down the street and I could tell by Flaco's expression something was wrong. As the car passed, I noticed it was full of gang bangers. Flaco didn't look behind us as the car passed, he just said, "Listen Chris, when we turn the corner run fast. If these fools catch you, they'll kill you."

I looked behind me at the car, which was now stopped in the middle of the street. One guy had his head out the window looking back at us. My heart started pumping...as soon as we turned the corner, we broke into a straight run. As we're running, Flaco yells that we need to split up, get to a phone to call Dina, and tell her we're being chased by some fools from Travelers, and we have no guns.

Flaco jumped the fence. I saw a good hiding spot and hid. Not more than a second later I heard footsteps on the pavement. They ran right past me and went over the fence. I hid there with my heart pounding in my chest! I hid for at least ten minutes. Then I stood up, brushed myself off, and slowly walked out to the street. I ended up on Harbor Blvd. Across the street was the Anaheim Police station, where I felt safe... but was I wrong.

As I walked down Harbor towards Katella, I see that same car coming from the opposite direction. They were mad dogging me as they passed. Being so close to the police station,

I didn't think they would try anything. They made a U-turn, and as they approached me, I saw a gun come out of the window. I jumped behind a car just in time because those fuckers shot at me!!!

I couldn't believe it. I started walking, thinking they're coming back... when I hear Flaco yelling at the intersection. I ran to Dina's truck and jumped in the back. We drove to Flaco's parents' house. This was just the first of many incidents.

Flaco's family was totally different compared to mine. They accepted him no matter what he was involved with. His family even accepted me, in a way. They were always offering me food whenever I was at their house. I always wondered what my life would've been like if my parents had not been different.

After we ate, we drove back to Dina's apartment. The sun would set soon, and we had to check on Dina. There always had to be someone there to protect her from being robbed. There are plenty of cliques roaming Orange County looking for drug dealers to rob.

When we walked through Dina's front door there were a few guys sitting on her couch. I knew one of them, Bully. He ran around the Rio Visto and Lincoln area. I didn't know the other one. Bully was always beating up people because he could. Straight dope we never got along. Dina was selling dope to more people around the area all the time. I was shocked when I saw Bully because of the problems I had in his area.

As I walked through to the living room to get something to drink out of the kitchen, Bully said, "Why you guys have this idiot round here for?" I just ignored him and kept going as I've never liked his style.

A few minutes later I heard Bully leaving and it was then that Flaco and Chico came into the kitchen and jumped me. When they stopped, I felt blood coming out of my nose. I could taste it on my lips. Dina came running into the kitchen.

"What's going on?" Dina cried.

"It's none of your business Dina. Go back upstairs." Flaco

replied.

Dina looked at me, then walked out of the kitchen, as Flaco sat me down in a chair. "Listen Chris. I warned you about letting people disrespect you like that! You'll never make it on the streets like this. Take this as a lesson. We've all learned something the hard way. Next time someone disrespects you walk up to them and start swingin'. I'll be right behind you and Chico behind me. But if you don't stick up for yourself, no one will respect you. I know people have been running all over you. It stops here."

"Of course I will Flaco."

"Okay then Chris. This is it! It stops here. We need to be down for us!" Flaco replied. Flaco looked at me for a second then shook my hand. He started to walk away but stopped, "Look Chris, we've got love for you, don't forget that." I lit a smoke and sat there for a second.

I went into the bathroom, flicked my smoke in the toilet, and then washed the blood off my face. I remember that day like yesterday. The odd part was I finally had some friends that cared. As crazy as that sounds, it was true.

That night Flaco came down the stairs with clippers in his hand. "You gotta cut your hair homie." That only took five minutes. I didn't like the buzz cut much. Dina walked in the kitchen and smiled at me. I stood up to go take a shower and as I walked out of the kitchen I heard Dina say, "Flaco, you're corrupting Chris."

"It's for his own good, Dina. If he's going to be running around these streets he has to be able to take care of himself."

"I know," Dina added. "I just hate to see him become like all of us."

After I showered I went back downstairs. Flaco, Chico, and Matt were laughing at Little Kenny. He kept trying to do handstands, which weren't working out well.

"Matt, you're staying around tonight, right?" Flaco asked.

"Yeah, Homie." Matt replied, "You guys leaving or what?"

"Yeah, we're going to look for a few people."

Flaco went upstairs to grab a couple of guns. "You look

totally different with your hair chopped off," Matt commented.

"I feel different too," I answered.

When Flaco returned he had a 357 revolver and a semi-automatic 45. He handed the 357 to Chico who put it in his pocket.

I never carried a gun unless I had to transport it to a certain location. These guys carry guns like packs of smokes. It was Matt's night to watch the pad. Someone always stayed around packing a gun. We drove down the alley to Greg's apartment. Dina wanted us to deliver some dope to him.

Greg was an older white guy who sold meth for extra money. If you saw him you'd be shocked to find out he sold dope. He worked all day, came home, and sold drugs at night very much like my dad did.

When we arrived at the end of the alley, Greg was working in his garage. We all stepped out of the truck to talk to him.

"You three look like you're up to no good," Greg said casually with a smile on his face.

"What gives you that impression Greg?" Flaco asked.

Greg laughed a little. "I guess it's Chris's new haircut and his black eye. What happened, Chris?"

"Well, I..."

"He got into a fight earlier. No big deal." Chico finished for me.

Flaco reached into his pocket and pulled out an ounce of meth, handed it to Greg, then told him Dina would be by later to pick up the cash. Greg acknowledged, shook hands with him and we left.

We drove down East Street heading towards Lincoln Ave. To the same neighborhood where I had been shot at. When we arrived, it was a little after 9 PM.

"We're going to look for these guys who shot at you." Flaco said.

"Are you scared?" Chico started laughing.

"Hell NO!" I replied.

"We probably won't even find any of them, or their homeboys. So, we'll go shopping for some stereos." Flaco added.

When we stepped out of the truck I looked up and down the street, just to make sure. Having a gun in my pocket didn't sound bad at this point. As we began walking down the street, Flaco and Chico were clowning around with each other like they had no fear at all.

Car lights lit up the night and we all jumped behind another car as it slowly passed us. Luckily it kept going.

"Fuck this shit, Homies! I'm bored. Let's go shopping!" Flaco demanded.

All three of us started scouring the neighborhood for nice cars with nice rims. Most of the time these nice cars have expensive stereo systems in them. Furthermore, they are usually owned by gang bangers.

It didn't take long for Chico to give a low whistle which stopped Flaco and me in our tracks. Chico discovered a Nissan lowered truck with nice rims and all.

When I approached, Flaco and Chico were already figuring out how to break in. There was an LCD light blinking on the dashboard.

"Get under the truck and clip the hot wire going to he battery. That should disable it." Flaco explained.

"Fuck, homie." Chico replied as he pulled himself under the car to find the hotwire leading to the battery. We were both quiet, watching the little light, and a minute later the light stopped.

Flaco shattered the window, and was inside the car within ten seconds, working on the stereo. I just kept looking up and down the street. Being that it was late the chances of getting caught were not very high.

"Hurry up Flaco," Chico whispered, "just steal the whole truck, it's quicker!"

"Calm down!" Flaco replied.

A minute later Flaco started handing us stereo equipment. He got an Alpine stereo, amplifier, and 2-12" speakers.

"About time homeboy." Chico said.

"Yeah, thanks for all your help." Flaco remarked.

We walked back to Dina's truck and headed back to the apartment. It was about 1:30 AM when we walked through the sliding glass door.

When we got back to the apartment, two people were lounging around and Flaco asked who they were. One said his name was Joker and the other was Kristle. They said they were waiting for Matt, who was upstairs with Dina.

Joker was crazy looking with tattoos on his arms and over his eyebrows. Kristle was hot with long straight blonde hair. I couldn't stop looking at her. She couldn't have been over 18. About that time Matt walked into the kitchen.

He said he was glad we were back because he was going to Garden Grove for a while. He said he'd be back tomorrow night. They all stood up and walked out the sliding glass door. Flaco stared at the door, and then said, "I don't trust Matt. People are coming from all over the place to buy dope from here. Someone is eventually going to try and rob Dina."

"Well, talk to Dina about it." I suggested.

"I did Chris, but she won't listen!"

I followed Flaco into the living room as I could see how very concerned he was. He left to go upstairs and talk to Dina. When he was halfway up the stairs, he stopped, "Chris, we've got to be more careful around here with all the money lying around, and most importantly, Little Kenny. Matt is bringing all these hinky people from all over the county. It's too sketchy."

He continued up the stairs. I locked all the doors and sat down on the couch. I wasn't on the couch two minutes before I could hear Dina and Flaco arguing.

Flaco came down the stairs mumbling to himself. He told me that he and Chico had to leave to talk to their homeboys. I was to always keep the gun on me. They'd be back in the morning.

Flaco and Chico are from the same gang. They call themselves "Anaheim Pauline Street" (Evil Pauline) which is located on the Eastside of Anaheim. Being part of a gang always sounded kind of strange to me. Yet, here I was now, running the streets with violent gang members.

Most times I felt out of place at Dina's. Dina came down the stairs and sat next to me on the couch. She handed me a meth pipe and asked if I wanted some. Smoking meth was all I did it seemed.

"Sure," I said, "I've been known to smoke a little speed."

"Why did Flaco jump you in the kitchen?"

"Bully, who had been here buying some speed that day, disrespected me, and I just ignored him... so they jumped me."

"Well, they're right Chris. You must stand up for yourself on the streets, or people like Bully will walk all over you."

This was the first time we really talked. It was just the two of us. Usually, she was busy talking to someone about dealings, usually about dope. Little Kenny was upstairs sleeping. We talked for a couple of hours. I explained to her the whole story about my childhood and a few other things. When we were finished, she told me that her brother was being released from jail in a few days.

"His name's Willy. He's kind of a knucklehead (meaning trouble on the streets) but with things like they are right now, it would be a good idea to have him around," she explained.

She also explained that Little Kenny was asking for me. I wanted to tell her how hard it was for Little Kenny to grow up in an environment like this, but I'm sure she already knew.

Dina was nice to me, but I'd seen her be tough with others. I kicked off my shoes and laid down on the couch.

It felt like just as I laid down, I heard Little Kenny begging me to get up, and he wouldn't stop. The sun was up and so was Kenny. He kept yelling for me to get up. Finally, I grabbed him and tickled him half to death because he was getting on my nerves. After I had done that my stomach felt like it was in a knot. So, I put on some cartoons for him and asked if he was hungry, and his answer was yes, "Pancakes, Pancakes," He yelled from the living room.

Before I started cooking pancakes I went to the closet where my belongings were and grabbed my toothbrush, washed my face, reached into my pocket for my bag of meth, and dumped a little on the sink. I chopped and snorted it in about three seconds. Now I was ready to make some pancakes for the little guy.

I started to wonder what would happen to Kenny, if Dina got busted. My mom got me out of my dad's house just in time. I thought I had the coolest dad, but I didn't realize until years later, what an awful thing my dad had done, starting me on drugs, and now my life was a disaster. The worst part was I had no one to help me. By the time I was ready to change my lifestyle, my family didn't want me around. Mom's boyfriend didn't even want me in the house. My dad's girlfriend made it impossible to be around them. I had so much resentment towards them from the past it was difficult to continue a normal relationship. I felt like running the streets was all that I had.

I remember serving a 90-day jail sentence for possession of an illegal knife. I kept telling myself that I had to get off the streets. If I didn't change my lifestyle I would end up in prison, possibly even dead. I'm not stupid. Everyone around me was in a gang, spent time in prison or was currently in prison and proud of it. That was going to be my life.

Being released from prison, or being on parole, were things that didn't seem to matter to those around me. This was just their normal way of thinking. I was far from someone who would kill or think this lifestyle was something to be proud of. I was definitely raised in a situation that turned me into a bad drug addict. No one really cared for me after my parents got a divorce, and all my role models were drug addicts, so I never really cared.

One day I was walking on the little yard, listening to the inmates talk about this program that sounded interesting. I knew that if I didn't get help I would be lost forever. So, I wrote a letter to the program. I was able to get accepted but not on the day of my release, which was a Thursday. They would only accept me on te following Monday. A lot could happen in those few days.

I was released at 12 AM. We drove out the gates at almost 2 in the morning. Just my luck I had become sick. I got this guy who was released with me to give me a ride to my mom's. Sure, I could've called Dina to send someone to pick me up; but I really wanted to try and straighten my life out now. I was becoming out of control like the rest of my friends.

When I arrived at my mom's apartment, it was 3 in the morning. Rain was pouring down on the streets. I had to knock like ten times to get an answer. Finally, my mom opened the door. I explained to her about just being released from jail, and that I was going into a program on Monday. I was really sick, I told her, and needed a place to stay until Monday.

"Hold on and let me ask Bill."

I thought to myself, *Your boyfriend has no job, you pay the bills, he spends your money, why in the hell would you have to ask him if your son could stay or not?*

Mom returned, "Bill says you can't stay." I just looked at her confused. Was this really happening?

I didn't say a word, I just turned on my heels and left! I never wanted to kill anyone in my life until that night in the pouring rain. I sat on the curb trying to think of a place to go until Monday. I was so cold my teeth were chattering.

By the time this was happening, Dina and I had become close. She looked out for me, even if I was wrong. I finally told myself I had nowhere else to go; and certainly, had to get out of the rain.

I called Dina telling her that I had been released from jail and was off Tustin Ave., in the City of Orange.

"What's wrong, Chris?"

"I'll explain later. Could you come pick me up? I'm soaked from the rain."

Fifteen minutes later Dina drove up. It was kind of sad to imagine that someone I've only known for about a year was more concerned about me than anyone in my family.

She asked me how I got to where she was picking me up. I explained that I bummed a ride from a guy who had been released with me.

On the way back to her pad I explained the whole story to Dina. My life changed forever that night. I totally stopped caring about everything. My only concern was the people who were close to me, which were the people on the streets. I never made it to that program on Monday, and I never looked back.

The streets in and around Anaheim could be unforgiving, and the days ahead were tough. I learned a lot of hard lessons that changed me, making me a lot tougher along the way.

One night as I was hanging around the pad, the phone rang. It was Flaco. He asked me, "What's up, dawg?" He continued to explain that he and Chico got cracked and were in jail. He said they found a shotgun and some dope. "I'll find Dina, don't trip. Do you have bail?"

"Yeah, it's ten thousand dollars."

"Okay, I'll find her and let her know."

Later that night Dina walked through the door. Matt and I were smoking meth in the kitchen. All night Matt suggested we go to Garden Grove to meet up with Kristle. Dina ended up leaving with Little Kenny to her friend's house. So, we locked up the pad and headed to Garden Grove.

We stayed at Kristle's until the sun came up, getting high. Kristle was cool, and super hot.

Joker had just been released from Prison. He was a trip. He looked a little unstable to me. Tattoos over his eye brows, and up and down his arms. He spent all his life in and out of prison.

I said to myself, *I'll never be like this guy.*

The following morning when we came through Dina's front door, Flaco and Dina were having a serious conversation on the couch. They were trying to figure out why Flaco's bail was set at ten thousand, while Chico's bail was only five thousand. It didn't make sense to Dina. She suggested that Chico must have ratted on him, and Dina was adamant about it. Flaco was angry for Dina even suggesting something like that to him. Yet, a few days later when Flaco received the police report, Chico had in fact told on Flaco. Flaco was angry but hurt more than anything. Flaco and Chico were close. We didn't see Chico at the pad after that happened. We heard stories that he was around, but he never came near us.

Life went on for the rest of us. We sold meth, smoked meth,

and ran the streets at all hours of the night. Dina's pad became so unpredictable that nothing surprised me anymore. People were being stabbed or beat on a daily basis.

One day I grabbed one of the cars and took off to go see Suzy. I would always go steal her from her boyfriend. We had drifted apart. I still loved her like never before things were just messed up.

When I arrived, she was out front with her dad by his camper. She saw me drive up and met me at my car. She explained that she was moving to Missouri with her dad. Thinking to myself, what? I couldn't even find the words to say anything. What could I say? I was bummed out. I was so messed up on drugs that it really didn't hit me until later.

One time I started driving to her house and realized half way there that she was gone. I will never forget that moment. Later that day I received a call from Matt on my pager. When I called him back, he was all tweeked out, "Chris, is it you?"

"Yeah, what's up?"

"Don't go back to the apartment. Someone was stabbed on the front lawn. We'll be at the Day's Inn, Hotel."

The Day's Inn became our home for the next month. Little Kenny had his toys all over the place. He acted like nothing had happened and went with the flow. I just sat in the chair by the back window, staring out into the parking lot, wondering what was next.

This Hotel was off the 91 freeway. It would actually be a good place to sell drugs out of, and that's exactly what we did for the next month.

With all the different groups running the streets, you couldn't keep up. They mostly all did meth. So, I started meeting all sorts of new people.

One day as I am looking out the window, I see my homeboy's arguing in the back parking lot. They had just left the hotel room to meet someone to sell them some meth. I thought, *oh no,* knowing what was about to happen. Right after I finished that thought one of my buddies jumped in his car as the other guy took off running through the parking lot. He started chasing this guy in Dina's car, catching him, and running him over with the car. I just shook my head. I started packing all of our belongings. We'd be moving again.

A couple days later we landed at the Tampico Motel off State College and Lincoln. It was a rundown motel where all the tweekers lived and hung out. It wouldn't be a place we'd stay long.

As we were all sitting around bored and spun out on meth, Matt and Flaco were arguing. Flaco was certain Matt wouldn't have the heart to shoot someone. And Flaco was calling Matt out on it. Matt started to get nervous knowing Flaco was serious. As they're arguing I see Little Kenny looking at them.

Next thing I know I hear a gun shot, and Flaco is holding his foot lying on the motel floor, in some serious pain. Matt shouts, "Oh shit!" Claiming that he thought the gun was empty, as Flaco rolls around on the floor.

Dina says, "We got to get out of here in case someone heard the gunshot. We'll never be able to explain this to the cops." As Dina helped Flaco he mumbled to Dina, "Take me to my parent's." Dina didn't even reply as she walked out of the motel room. Everyone started packing all our stuff. We didn't even last the night at this place. I was getting sick of moving all the time.

# CHAPTER 7

The next place we landed at was The Diznavu, off Harbor Blvd. We lasted a lot longer at that location.

The owner was Middle Eastern and extremely helpful to our business. If the police called the hotel asking questions, he'd let us know. The Anaheim police always came nosing around hotels and motels, asking or looking for people just like us.

Our room was in the very back, perfect for selling dope. The actual size of the rooms was not that big, with two beds, a little table with two small chairs by the window (facing the parking lot) and the door right next to the window. The bathroom had a shower crammed in there. Since this place was only temporary, it would work.

Disneyland was only five minutes away. But the worst part was the Anaheim Police Department was just five minutes in the other direction. The surrounding area was gang infested and full of scandalous people. Its been cleaned up since the early 90s, but still dangerous. Dina's brother, Willy had been released from jail. He was a big ass whiteboy, and tough as hell. I knew he was dangerous right when I met him. It didn't take long for Willy to find trouble.

One night Flaco and I were smokin' meth, bored to death in our hotel room. When Dina received a call from her brother. I could see Dina getting upset as she talking to Willy. When Dina hung up the phone she was irate. She started to explain how her brother had been jumped by Bully and his friends and was at 7-Eleven. Flaco says, "We'll go get him." As he grabs the 357 revolver off the nightstand.

As we're walking out the front door I said, "Here we go again."

Flaco couldn't get there quick enough. When we drove up Willy was out front of the store on the curb smoking a cigarette. I looked around but didn't spot Bully, or his friends. Flaco was unpredictable, plus it was crowded. People were everywhere. It could've been a disaster.

When we returned to the hotel Willy and Dina started arguing about some sibling crap. I gave Flaco a look and was out the door. I was sick of all the drama surrounding Dina. I decided to go see a friend at her house. Michele spent a lot of time there and I hoped to see her. I'd always liked Michele but when I made my way through her house smoking meth, Michele wasn't there, so I left.

When I arrived back at the hotel Dina was all excited about a house she rented, right down the street. It had three bedrooms, two baths, and a nice backyard for Little Kenny. We were so worried about being robbed that we hooked a motion detector in the front yard. When somebody came walking up to the pad a light would come on in the living room.

That house didn't last long. Not even a week later I get a call on my pager from Matt. When I called him, I was shocked to hear what he had to say. "Willy was just arrested by some plain clothes detectives from the Anaheim Police department. They came storming into the pad with all their guns and shit. There was a scale, dope, and some other stuff lying around. They didn't even trip on it."

"What did they arrest him for Matt?" I replied.

Matt paused on the line for a second, and said, "Bully was murdered. And I guess they think he did it."

I sat at the payphone watching cars drive and said, "Matt, nothing will ever be the same. I'm on my way there. Stay until I get there."

"Hurry the hell up," Matt cried, "I'm getting out of here for a few days."

"Alright, just wait for me. Where is Dina?"

"She took Little Kenny to Greg's to try and figure all this shit out."

"Matt, I need a gun." I replied and hung up the phone. I knew nothing would ever be the same.

Apparently, when the Anaheim Police raided Dina's house, they came in looking for only one person, Willy. Bully was found lying in the street off State College Blvd. with a gunshot wound. Bully was rushed to the hospital where he later died of his injuries.

This incident created all kinds of problems for all of us living with Dina. Friends started taking sides, creating problems. All Bully's homies were talking about revenge against Mike, Dina, and even me. At this point I could care less. With my gun in my pocket I felt untouchable. I knew I would end up in prison or dead if I didn't wise up.

My family and friends I grew up with had given up on me. The only family I had now was Dina, and my homeboys who I ran the streets with. They loved me no matter if I was right or wrong, high or sober.

Later on, after everything had calmed down, I traveled from house to house buying time with this guy Jack. I stopped at this girl's house, Renee. Located off St College Blvd. and South Street. We were all smoking meth and having a good time. Next thing I know Jack leaves, saying he'll be back later. Well, he never came back. Renee and I talked all night.

Renee was just a couple years older than I was, with long blonde hair, brown eyes, and really good looking. Renee also had a one-year-old son named Cory. Whose father was off doing his own thing.

As the sun came up the following morning I headed back to Dina's. I felt really happy meeting Renee. As I walked through the door Dina asked, "Where have you been?"

"At Renee's house."

Dina looked at me with a curious look and replied, "Who's Renee?"

I started to explain and Dina went off on the night's event. I could tell she wasn't happy about it. I don't know, but it felt awkward.

I noticed Dina had all these boxes stacked in the corner, and before I could ask, Dina started to explain we were moving again. The new house was only a mile away. The neighborhood was actually a little nicer.

By this time Dina and Flaco had split up. Flaco started hanging out with his homeboy's, and we stopped running the streets together. It was too late for me. Flaco had turned me into a person I thought I would never be. Running around with a gun everywhere, shooting at people only to prove I was harder than the next guy. I had just turned 23.

Renee and I fell in love over the weeks. And it wasn't long before I moved in with her at her parent's house. Her parents Rich and Rhianna, were both understanding of my situation. Rhianna made me laugh. Before she really knew me she asked Renee, "Who's that Mexican guy coming over here all the time?"

"Mom! That's Chris, and he's white."

I'd been hanging around Flaco so long I dressed like a gang banger. White T-shirts, baggy pants creased real nice, and a 'I don't give a fuck' attitude.

Matt had been sent to prison for possessing a firearm and Dina went to prison right behind him for selling drugs. Our whole crew seemed to have fallen apart. With Dina, Flaco, and the rest of our crew gone, I couldn't trust many people.

I started spending a lot of time at Kristle's. We'd become good friends. Then her boyfriend was paroled from prison, and we became buddies fast. Luckily, Chucky Normad (Kristle's boyfriend), and me were two of the best crime partners that ran together. Chucky was down for anything, and I couldn't of asked for a better friend.

I never brought Renee around my friends because I always had a gun and never knew what could happen. But I came home most nights if I had time.

I became consumed by the streets. It was like I had something to prove all the time. That I was tougher, and crazier than the next guy. With Dina gone I wanted everyone to know that I didn't need her, or Flaco, or anyone for the matter. And Chucky fueled the fire.

One day we're delivering meth off Beach Blvd, when I spotted a truck delivering packages to houses. I look over at Chucky, "If that lame leaves his truck running, I'm takin' it."

On the streets we call people who are not in the game lames, squares, etc.

As usual when I told Chucky I am taking the truck, he didn't say anything. The quietest person I ever met.

Not even a minute after we're following this truck, the truck driver jumps out and walks up to a house with a package. I jump out of Chucky's car and run towards the truck, jump into the driver's seat, and drive off. I drove as fast as possible in this big delivery truck and park it about a mile from the scene. Chucky drives up, et in Dawg! We'll come back later."

Chucky sped off with my heart pounding in my chest.

"Dawg!" Chucky says, "We need to split up. The cops will be looking for two people."

I jump out of the car on Ball Rd. With a backpack full of dope, gun, bullets, and some other stuff. I notice this long-haired guy walking on the other side of the street. He was heading towards the AM/PM Mini Mart across the street from the Jack & Jill motel. I had to get off the streets for a while.

I ran across the street to catch up with this guy (maybe he lived close by). As he walked out of the AM/PM. I caught up with him, "Hey, can I talk to you a second?"

He gave me a weird look, "Sure, what's up?"

"My name is Chris. Do you use Meth?"

He looked at me even weirder this time and slowly

responded, "Yeah, why?"

"Look, I need a place to hang out until my homeboy can come pick me up. I'll get you high if you help me out."

He looked at me for a second then replied, "Yeah, I can help you out. But the cops aren't chasing you are they?"

"No, why would you say that?"

"I just had to ask. Follow me Chris. I live just around the corner."

As I'm following down the street I already felt relieved. His house was only a minute's walk from AM/PM.

I told Chucky, "Hey homeboy! Guess what?"

"Chris, what happen' now?"

"Nothing Dawg. But I found a whole group of tweekers to sell dope to and a house to sell it out of."

As luck would have it Jenna was renting a room in the front of the house. The best part about this room is you can see the front of the house through the bedroom window and see who's coming up the driveway.

Two hours later me, Chucky and Kristle were moving our belongings into the pad. I was excited about this new pad. It brought back memories of Dina and my old crew. Not even an hour after we moved in there, there was a knock at the bedroom door. "Who is it?" I yelled.

"It's me Chris, Jenna."

"Come in," I replied.

Jenna was my new landlord. She seemed to be an okay girl. Maybe 40 years old, brown hair, and brown eyes. With her glasses, she reminded me of a librarian.

"What's up Jenna?"

"This guy Aron wants to buy an ounce of Meth" I looked at Chucky and asked, "Do you know this guy, or heard of him?"

Chucky and Kristle shake their heads. "Jenna, is this guy by himself?" "Yeah, he's sitting out front in his car," Jenna explained.

"Well, tell him to come in."

"He said he'd rather not."

I looked at Chucky for some kind of a sign of what to do.

When Chucky obviously left it up to me, I picked up my gun, clicked off the safety, placed it in my waistband, grabbed an ounce of dope and headed out front.

Parked out front was a Mazda RX7, with this Aron guy watching me approach his car. As I came closer to his car, I placed my hand on my gun under my shirt. I didn't waste no time. "You got $650 bucks, Aron?"

"Sure do." He replied.

Aron hesitates like he's leery of me. I lifted up my shirt and said, "Look, if I was gonna burn you, I would've already done it."

I see Aron thinking, then he reaches in his pocket and pulls out a wad of cash. It looked like $650 bucks to me. I grabbed the wad of cash, throw the ounce of dope on his seat, and what happened next caught me by surprise.

Aron pops the clutch in his car, taking off, screeching tires and all. My first thought was he's trying to burn me. So, I pull out my gun and start shooting at him as he turns the corner. I got three shots off.

I put the gun back down my pants, then looked around to see if anyone was watching me. This was the middle of the afternoon. I slowly walked back into the house like nothing happened, until I came face to face with my landlord. Jenna was standing inside as I stepped through the door, eyes wide open.

"Jenna! Why is your buddy shooting at me?" I cried.

"What happened, Chris?" Jenna asks.

I looked at her and said, "Really couldn't tell you Jenna."

Then went straight to my room shutting the door behind me. Chucky was already packing up the backpacks. Kristle looks at me, "Chris, did you shoot that guy?"

I picked up my backpack and replied, "Maybe. I tried. Here Chucky, count the money."

Chucky laughs, "Hey fool! It's only five dollars short. Why'd you shoot at him?"

"I don't know. He took off like he's burnin' me or something. So I started shooting at him."

A minute later we're loading up the car and Chucky say's "Dawg, You just shot at a guy over $5. How could I not love you."

Later that night we went back to the pad to see what's up. Again, soon as I stepped through the door Jenna was waiting, "Chris, you can't live here."

I gave her an innocent look and replied, "Why, Jenna?"

"Chris, you know why."

I looked at Chucky and started to laugh. I couldn't help it. "Well Jenna, I guess I'll grab the rest of our stuff and be on my way."

I had Chucky drop me off at Renee's house. I promised I would watch this movie with her called "Speed" that had just come out on video. As we're watching Renee stands up and pauses the movie.

"Why'd you do that babe?" Thinking that I was in trouble or something.

"I wanna talk to you about something, calm down." Renee says. "My parents bought a house in Lake Havasu, Arizona. Do you know where that's at?"

"Of Course I do." I said with a sarcastic look on my face.

"Well, my mom asked if you, me, and Cory wanna move out there until they retire. We could save and get our own place later on."

Until Renee said this to me I didn t realize how serious our relationship was. I sat there shocked, then replied, "How long till they move out there?"

"Two months, maybe more."

I started forming all these thoughts in my mind. *Get out of Anaheim and get off drugs? Why shouldn't I do this?* I said to myself. I never had an opportunity like this to leave Orange County. "You know what Renee, let's do it."

Renee kissed me with a big smile on her face and started the movie again.

# CHAPTER 8

Lake Havasu was totally different than Anaheim. Thousands of college kids, and families vacation there during spring break. There were no gangs or anything of that nature. I knew I would need a motorcycle, or something to pass the time, so I started looking right away.

My first toy was a red go-kart. Not your normal one either. It was equipped with a Briggs & Stratton motor with five horse power, disk brakes, slick tires, and if you wanted, you could fit it with a racing motor.

The go-kart was slow to start but when it hit top speed, it was fast. You could turn any corner at top speed. I'm guessing it's because of the slick tires. I found trouble with it in no time.

A couple of days after I purchased the go-kart, I needed gas for it. Since I had no gas can, I drove to the nearest gas station, located about a half mile down South St. First, I needed to get high before I went on this little mission, so I went inside to smoke a little meth. Then I was out the back door. I heard Renee yell for me but I ignored her.

South St., the street that Renee lived on, had a gas station at the first light, driving towards Disneyland, coming from St. College. It should be no trouble at all.

As I drove my go-kart through the back streets with a cigarette in my mouth, black hat turned backward, thinking I am the coolest person in Anaheim, I didn't have a care in the world. I was actually having a good time, making my way through the side streets with no problems.

A couple of kids waved excitedly as I flew by them. When I actually drove onto South St., I only had a minute until the gas station appeared. No problem, right? You'd think so. I get stuck at a 4-way light. The gas station was across the street on the right-hand corner. It's the middle of the afternoon, and I have a few cars behind me. The rest of the intersection is clear. Until an Anaheim Police car pulls up to the red light, and my light is green. As we made eye contact I'm thinking to myself, *Son of a bitch!*

I flip a U-turn, right back the way I came from. Knowing my go-kart took time to gain speed I thought I would be caught. But as I quickly started racing through those back streets, I regained my confidence. Hugging every corner with no fear at all. Those same kids were waiting for me, trying to get me to stop as I flew by them. I yelled, "Cop's" and pointed behind me. The next corner would lead me right to Renee. As I drove up her driveway, I slammed the brakes on, slid onto the grass and spun out. I jumped out of the seat, grabbed the front of the go-karts frame and dragged it inside the backyard through the side gate. I sat on the ground and lit a smoke. "Son of a bitch!"

I had to laugh a little about ditching a cop on a go-kart. I stood up slowly to peek through the gate. If they pulled up out front I would start hopping fences because I had a warrant for my arrest.

Sure enough an Anaheim Police car slowly drove by no doubt upset about letting a go-kart get the best of him. Renee came out the back door with Cory in her arms "Chris, what are you trippin' on? Go to sleep!"

"Renee, I just ditched a cop in my go-kart, and he just

drove by." I explained, so I didn't look like a total tweeker.

She just gave me a "Whatever" look as she slammed the door behind her.

Later that afternoon I received a call from Chucky. He explained he needed me to go to a few places with him. "Well, come get me dawg!" I replied as I grabbed some clean clothes and headed for the shower.

Once out of the shower I grabbed a piece of toilet paper, folded it in half, and dumped around a half gram of meth inside, folded it into a square, popped it in my mouth and washed it down with water. I'd be so high by the time Chucky arrived I'd be ready for anything.

I chased Cory down and started playing with him. As I had him pinned on the ground, I heard Chucky honk his car horn, so I handed Cory to Renee and muttered, "I'll be back later," as I gave her a kiss.

"Chris, don't get busted." Renee cried.

"Renee, don't say things like that. You'll jinx me."

As soon as I shut the car door behind me, Chucky says, "Did you eat meth again? You sweatin' like crazy." I pulled out my Tech-9 and replied, "Yep!" Chucky just shook his head.

This gun was dangerous, but never let me down. My Tech-9 had a 30-round clip, and once you pulled the pirate it would not stop firing rounds until the gun was empty. Dangerous sure, but what gun wasn't? As long as you kept control of it while firing rounds off, you were fine.

"Where we going?" I asked.

Chucky went on to explain that these two guys wanna buy a lot of meth, and they're from the West Side of Anaheim. And he'd feel better if I came with him. Their names were Josh and Cody, and they were at the Motel 6, near Disneyland.

Soon as we stepped through the door into their room I felt uneasy. We all introduced ourselves and sat down. Cody had what looked like a Mack-1O next to him. Cody looked at me and asked, "Chris, is it true you shot at Aron a few days ago?"

I thought for a second, where is this conversation leading? Were these guy's setting me and Chucky up? I had my gun on my lap knowing how fast this whole situation could get dangerous. Finally I replied, "Why, is he your homeboy, or what?"

"Yeah, I know him but it's not like that, Chris. I'm just curious."

"Does it really matter at this point, Cody? Let's talk about our business."

Josh cut our conversation off by talking to Chucky about some dope he wanted.

I started thinking as Chucky and Josh worked out their deal. First, I meet all these new tweeker's, and they're all connected to this Aron guy I shot at. All these new people were leaving a bad taste in my mouth, and I was starting to worry a little. I was happy to leave when Chucky stood up, shaking Josh's hand. I shook hands then followed Chucky out the front door. I mumbled to Chucky, "That was a little awkward, Dawg." Chucky looked at me and added, "Least they know who they're dealing with, right?"

"Yeah, well I have a bad feeling about these guys. I can't explain it, but they're trouble."

Once again Chucky stayed Chucky, leaving me to think about this whole situation myself.

As Chucky and I were delivering dope we stopped by an apartment in Fullerton. The guy looked like a straight square. You can clearly see he'd never done time in jail and probably never would. His apartment was real nice with new furniture, the works.

As Chucky and I are leaving this guy's apartment, he explains about this motorcycle he's selling. It's a Honda 600 XL. The ones that came out in the late 80s were nice. Next thing you know I work out a deal with him. I gave him $500 up front and would make payment for another $500. I'd take the bike to Lake Havasu with me.

Chucky and I went our separate ways. As I'm about to leave I received a page on my beeper. I was shocked to see Jenna's number across the pager's screen. I didn't even bother calling I drove right there.

Before pulling into the driveway I cruised by to see how many cars were parked there. The only one was a tan clunker, with a tall blonde just stepping out of her car. She looked to be about mid-20s with short hair, and super slim. She surely didn't look like she'd give any trouble, so I made a U-turn.

When I turned into Jenna's driveway, that blonde stopped to see who I was. As I'm taking off my helmet she walked up to me and asked, "Who are you?" With a curious look in her blue eyes, like I appeared from magic or something.

I paused before replying, "I'm Christopher Curtis."

"Oh yeah, I've heard of you. You're not going to shoot me are you?"

I laughed. I couldn't help it.

"My name is Emily." She added with pride.

"Emily, could you do me a favor and tell Jenna I'm out front."

Emily went inside without another word. As I'm waiting I couldn't stop thinking about this Emily. My thoughts were quickly interrupted when Jenna started to approach me. Jenna didn't waste no time asking if I had any meth for sale. Which was kind've a stupid question. Of course I did.

I followed her into the pad which was surprisingly empty compared to the last time I came through this door. Emily was smiling as she saw me. Before long Emily and me are talking about this and that. We wasted no time as I followed her to her apartment. Next thing I know, its morning, and I'm waking up naked in her bed, with her little sister standing in the doorway saying, "Cody is here, Emily."

I thought, "What!"

Emily explains to her sister not to let him in the apartment. And off she went down the hallway. The room was a mess. Clothes littered the floor. Posters hanging on all four walls, and the sun just starting to make its way through the bedroom curtains.

I quickly jumped up, grabbing my clothes to get dressed.

Then grabbed my Tech-9, thinking, *Could it really be that Cody I just met?*

"Emily, is Cody your boyfriend?"

"Look it didn't mean anything," she replied, "Yeah, but he's not coming in, so don't trip."

I thought to myself, *Well this is great. I might have to shoot this guy.* Knowing he had a gun, too. A minute later her sister comes back into the room saying Cody left. I grabbed my dope and quickly loaded my glass pipe with some meth and got high. I needed to get my head right.

The odd part about all this nonsense happening in my life, it wasn't always like this. Now after several years of running the streets I'm carrying guns, shooting at people, and not caring much about anything. I thought to myself, *If I could just make it to Lake Havasu, I'll change my life.*

Before I left Emily's pad, I got super high on meth. I must've eaten a half gram. Emily looked at me like I was insane when I poured meth into a piece of toilet paper and swallowed it. Why I decided to eat meth again, I don't know. It's never any good when I eat meth.

As I left her apartment, I drove down Harbor Blvd, coming from Disneyland. Who do I spot at the light across the street? Erik. With my helmet on, he has no idea it's me.

When the light turned green, I made a U-turn and followed him. It's early in the morning on a weekday. There's light traffic going our way. I decided I was going to scare the shit out of him.

As I pulled up beside him, I drew my Tech-9 from my waistband, and pointed it at his front tire, then pulled the pirate. Erik's face lit up with fear as my gun fired several shots, before jamming. This all happened in front of Disneyland.

I quickly sped up racing towards the 5 freeway. I needed to escape this area for a while. As I flew down the 5 freeway, heart pounding, I said to myself, *Why did I just do that? I ain't eating any more meth.* I ended up in Midway City, in Westminster, with Chucky and Kristle. I explained to Chucky what happened as Kristle walked up. "You did what!" Kristle replied, "Are you nuts!" I just smiled. I went on to explain about the girl I met the night before, and that I ate some meth before leaving. Chucky laughed, and added, "You shouldn't be eating meth for breakfast, Dawg." With a huge grin on his face. Chucky reached inside of his backpack, removing a 22 Berreta from inside. Then hands it to me. "Here Dawg. Sell that Tech-9. It's too dangerous."

I grabbed the gun from him. It practically fits in the palm of my hand. I removed the clip and all the bullets. I pop the spring out of the clip, cut off a piece of the spring, so I can load more bullets into the clip. Instead of just eight rounds, it now will hold ten rounds. I popped the clip in after reloading it, chambered a round, clicked the safety on, and slipped the gun in my front pocket. I was ready to go. You couldn't even tell I was carrying a firearm.

Westminster is no different than Anaheim, Garden Grove, Fullerton, or Santa Ana. The streets are full of gangsters and cops. Most cops are no different than the common criminal. They just have a badge that gives them free rein on all, with little or no consequences. I have no doubt that a cop will shoot you dead and make you look guilty.

After Dina went to prison I met all sorts of new people. It was like I broke through some kind of barrier, that held me to one group. Now I was all over the County. People were looking at me differently, too. Because when I first started running the streets I was bullied, robbed, and had no street smarts. Now I was out of control. It was like I pushed until something in my brain turned off. I just didn't care anymore. It was as if my mentality changed overnight. I'd either go to prison or be killed. And I was okay with that. I ended up just like everyone else, maybe even worse. I liked the high that came with carrying guns and robbing people. I felt like I couldn't be stopped.

In Westminster I met this guy Tony. His pad was off the 22 freeway and Beach Blvd. St, Tweeker' s hung around his apartment. I loved it.

His apartment had a garage hooked up with a couch, table, and carpet so we could hang out inside. The apartment was surprisingly clean.

Tony was raising two young kids on his own, and I respected him for that. He kept his kid's clothed and fed. Most importantly, he made sure his kids didn't see people smoking meth. I ended up staying most of the night at Tony's.

Renee had been paging me for hours by the time I decided to go home. I knew I better hurry. Renee was the only good thing in my life. I jumped on my motorcycle heading for the nearest freeway to get home.

I was dead tired when I arrived. The streets will wear you down. I grabbed some clothes and jumped in the shower. I'd have to explain to Renee why I didn't make it home last night. Every time I left lately, she looked at me like she wanted to cry. I always explained, "Don't worry, babe. I'll be alright."

"Honey, we're moving to Havasu soon. Please don't get arrested, or something."

I hung around the house for a while with Renee, before leaving on another mission. I could never sit still, I always felt like I was missing something.

As I was heading to Kristle's mom's apartment, I felt my pager vibrating in my pocket, so I checked it real quick. I was surprised to see Mick calling. I didn't see Mick much like I used too. I ran around with Mick before I even met Dina. I even looked up to Mick for a long time.

I met up with Mick at this girl's pad in Garden Grove. Next thing I know, we're driving all over the county in this girl's new Toyota Pathfinder. It was nice. Almost brand new. The last thing I remember was driving down the 22 freeway. Next thing I know I am on top of this brick wall, overlooking a cemetery. I jumped down from the wall, landing on the soft grass. Tombstones were only a couple feet away from me. Mick landed right next to me, saying, "Dawg, get that blood off your face."

Right then I felt wetness on my face, and the back of my head stung. "Mick, what's going on." I asked all confused.

Mick replied all nervous, "I fell asleep at the wheel and hit the center divider. And you were laying on the freeway when I got out of the truck. Then you jumped to your feet and started running, so I followed you."

I started trippin'. My heart was pounding in my chest. I felt for my gun, relieved to find it safely in my pocket, but my pager was gone. I couldn't believe it.

We started making our way through the cemetery. People were staring at us all weird. I felt weak and sick to my stomach. I told Mick to take me to Kristle's mom's pad and drop me off. We stopped at the nearest phone so Mick could call for a ride. When I arrived at Kristle's, Chucky and her were in the bedroom. Later they said I mumbled some story to them and fell asleep.

The next morning, I woke up a little dazed. The back of my head stuck to Kristle's pillow. Chucky and Kristle were gone. I reached for my pager then remembered it was gone. I thought to myself, *Mick almost got me killed yesterday.*

I stood up and headed for the shower. As I placed my head under the hot water it stung. I could see blood washing down the drain. I washed my wound as best as I could, then stepped out of the shower. I felt a whole lot better. So I went to the kitchen to find something to eat.

Kristle's mom, Laura was in the kitchen eating when I walked in, "Hi Laura." I mumbled as I grabbed some cereal.

"How you feeling?" She replied. Laura and I never really got along. I was hoping Kristle would walk through the front door. I felt awkward as I poured a bowl of cereal.

Every day seemed like a crazy story. I couldn't stop finding trouble. Like trouble was following me, or something.

A few days later I'm delivering some dope to Chuckey's buddy, who I purchased the motorcycle from. As I am knocking on the door a black girl answers. I said, "Oh excuse me. I've got the wrong apartment."

"Chris, is that you?" Chuckey's buddy yelled from inside the apartment.

"Yeah, it's me," I replied.

He came to the door explaining that this black girl was his wife. So I went inside and listened to these two talk my ear off. This girl wouldn't shut up about being a model, and how she just paid cash for this new car she bought. I couldn't believe Chucky was dealing with this dude, knowing his wife was black. Our friends would freak out if they heard about this.

As I'm leaving, I walk out to my motorcycle with this guy, and explain, "Look, you can't call us anymore. If our homeboy's found out about your wife being black, they'd trip on us." This guy gave me a funny look, and replied, "Okay Man."

I still owed this guy like $200 for the motorcycle and explained I would call him in a few days.

Days later I contacted him to pay him the rest of the money. He said for me to meet him at this Motel 6, so I let him know I was on the way.

I pull into the Motel 6 parking lot with no worries at all. I mean, what could happen, right? When I walked through the motel door, I felt a cold hard object in the middle of my back. Right away I knew it was a gun. "Put your hands up you racist piece of crap!" Some guy says to me from behind.

I thought to myself, *This dumb son of a bitch!*

I put my hands up and this guy who I bought the motorcycle from starts in on me, "Your friends don't like blacks."

I replied, "Just do what your gonna do."

They got my gun and all my money, and the motorcycle as they left. Soon as they left I called Chucky, and explained what had just happened. Chucky started laughing.

"Are you serious Dawg?" Chucky asked.

"Fuck yeah I'm serious. Come get me. Bring my backpack, and another gun."

Chucky showed up an hour later with Kristle. I walked out of the hotel mad, and embarrassed. I couldn't believe I let that happen to me. I was caught slippin'.

"Chucky take me to that lame's apartment."

Chucky already knew what time it was. This guy wasn't getting away with robbing me. As we drove to this guy's apartment, I ate a bunch of meth. Which only fueled my anger. I decided to catch his girl's new car on fire. That black girl was bragging about how she just bought her brand new Nissan Sentra for cash, and she hadn't even had time to insure it yet. As we pulled into the long alleyway, I reached into my backpack and pulled out a marble, and a flare gun. The marble would shatter the window, so I could shoot the flare gun off inside the car. It would catch that car on fire fast.

The alley was long with carports on each side and apartments overhead. The alley must've gone back ¼ of a mile. It was just about dark when we drove through the alley toward their carport.

Soon as Chucky stopped the car I jumped out, looking around to see if anyone was watching. Once I realized the coast was clear, I threw the marble at the car window, shattering it. With the flare gun I made a hole and shot a flare into the back seat of her new car. The Nissan lit up fast as I ran back to the car.

"Give me your cell phone, Chucky." I dialed the guy's number, and waited for him to answer, and said, "You better hurry up and go put the fire out in your new car." And hung up the phone. Chucky looked back at me in the backseat, and said, "You feel better, Dawg?"

As I gave him his phone back, I nodded, smiling as we left. The whole alley was glowing as we pulled onto the main street. I thought about all the apartments over the carport as we left. *Oops,* I said to myself.

Later that night that guy calls Chucky, explaining that he doesn't want no more problems, and he apologized. Chucky responded, "Just don't call the cops, and everything will be cool."

# PHOTO GALLERY

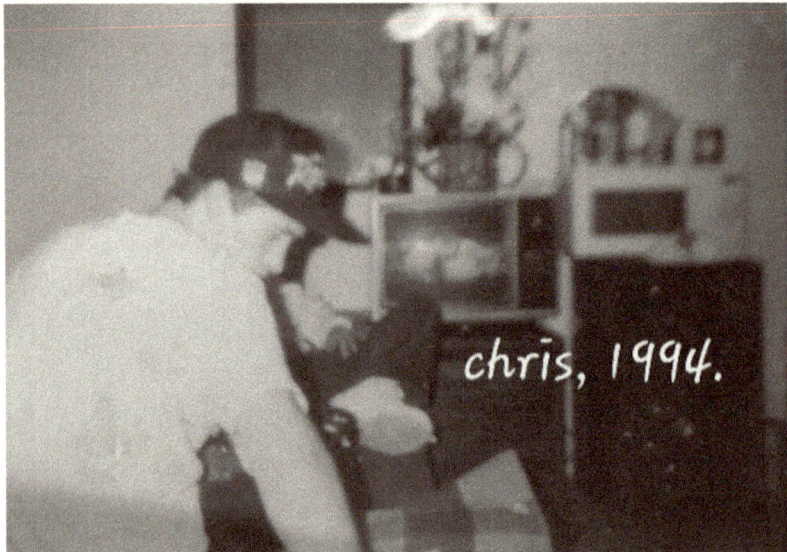

chris, 1994.

chris, 2002

chris, 2002.

chris. 2002.

chris. 2015.

chris, 2002.

chris, michele, and
kristle. 2022

chris, soledad. 2012

Chris, and Chucky. 2022

Chris, Michele, and
Chucky. 2022

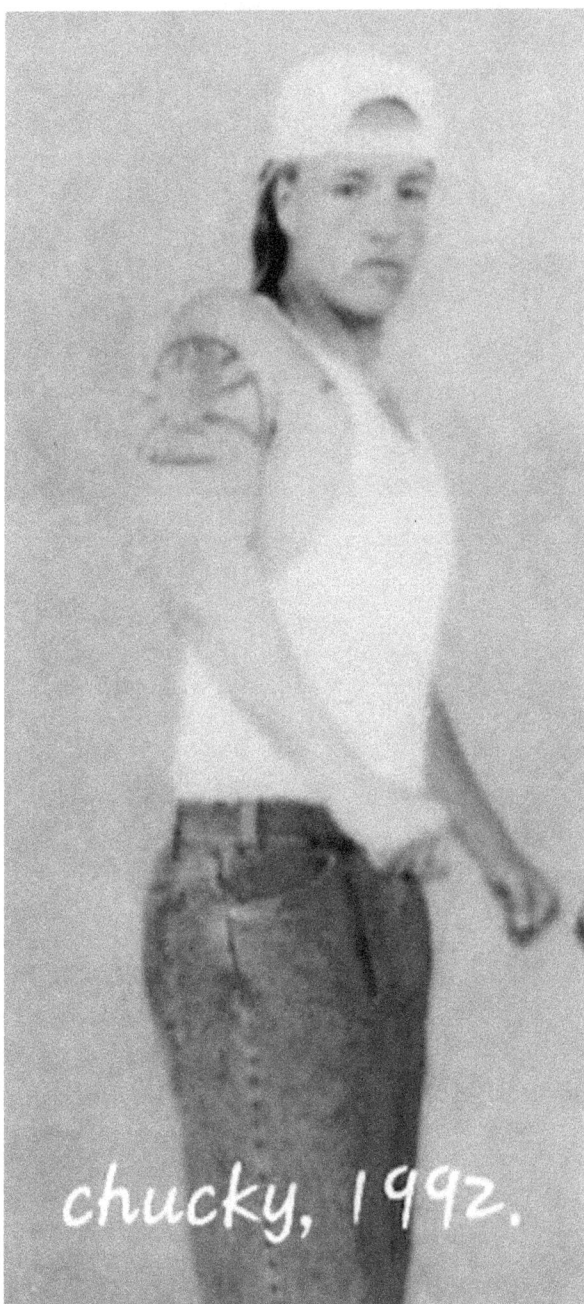
chucky, 1992.

Dad, 2002

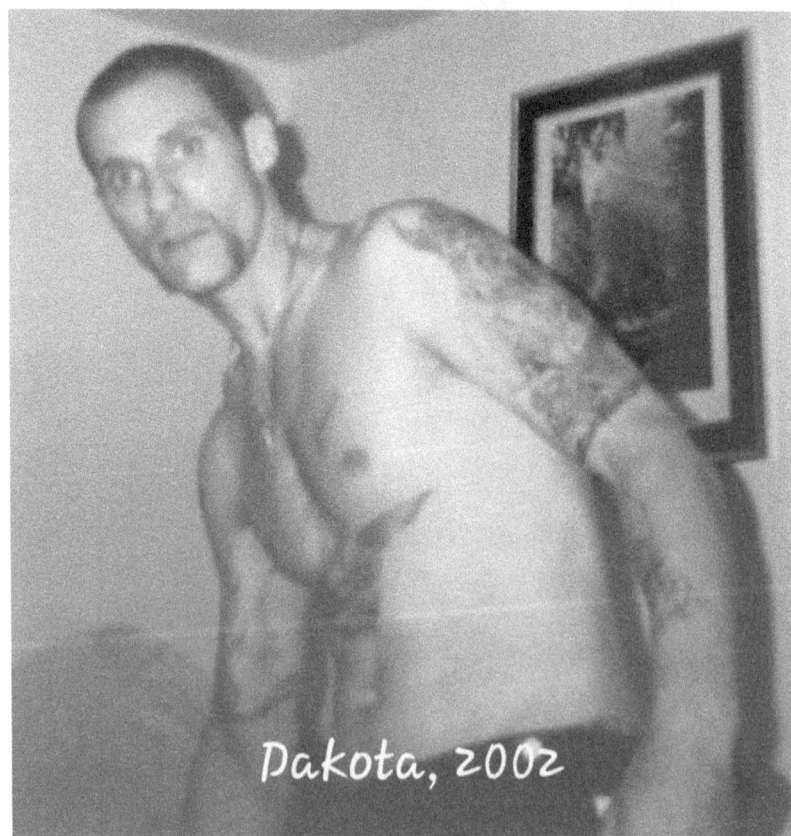
Dakota, 2002

Chris, and Michele.

1995

2022

Kristle, 1997.

Michele, and Brooke. 1996.

Michele, Brooke, and Chris. 2022.

Thank you for always supporting me mom. I love you.          m

Renee. 1996.

# CHAPTER 9

I rented a U-Haul van for the move to Lake Havasu, Arizona. We'd be moving real soon. I was eager to leave Orange County. I was in too deep, and this whole carrying guns and dealing drugs was a recipe for disaster. It was only a matter of time before someone was shot, maybe even me.

Renee and I loaded up all our belongings. She seemed excited to be finally leaving Anaheim. I won't lie; I was too. Lake Havasu was a nice place to live.

The first day in Havasu was full of mystery. With the dry hot air, rock filled front yards, and cactus growing everywhere, this place was nothing like Southern California. I was relieved to roam the streets without having to pack a gun. I felt brand new. I only brought an ounce of meth, and when it was gone, I'd quit.

Before leaving, Rich, Renee's dad, had run down all the rules to me. You know, the same rules parents always say. But he was adamant about one request.

"Chris, please don't get any motor oil on my new driveway."

"Rich," I replied sincerely, "I will take good care of your new house." And we shook hands.

On the first day Renee asked me to get some milk. "Sure babe," I replied. I was curious about my new surroundings. The sun was still hot, but not for long. I decided to ride a bike there. I'd race there and back in no time at all, right? Boy, was I wrong.

The ride to the market was all downhill. I quickly noticed the whole area was new homes. As I rode up to the store on my bike with my backpack on, people were coming and going with groceries, or buying gas. I received a few looks being dressed like a gang banger, but I didn't care.

I walked through the door and was blasted with cool air from the air conditioning. It felt good. I grabbed a gallon of milk and made my way to the candy section. I couldn't leave without a Butterfinger, my all time favorite candy bar. I looked out the front window noticing how fast the sun was setting. A few cars passed on the highway with their headlights on. Better hurry, I thought to myself. As I left the store on my bike it grew even darker. With no street lights I felt like I was in another world. It was strange being from another city where all you saw were lights at night. I couldn't see anything in no time at all. I even heard wings flapping overhead, which I'm guessing were bats flying around.

It took me passing a few streets before I realized I was lost. I had no clue where I was. I knew I lived on Pueblo Drive, but that's it. I started laughing to myself. I stopped and grabbed my big ass Motorola Brick phone and dialed Renee' number. I quickly realized I was out of range and was getting no signal.

"Son of a bitch!" I mumbled as I started pushing my bike up some unknown hill. As I am going uphill with my groceries, I felt like an idiot. I noticed a garage door open with a guy who looked like biker, long hair, beard, and oily clothes. I thought to myself, *This guy might be able to help me.* So, I made my way toward him.

"Excuse me, Sir."

He looked up at me with a curious look.

"I don't mean to bother you, but I just moved here and I am lost." I went to explain how I went to get milk and how it all went bad. The guy laughed at me and walked up to me to shake my hand. "My name is Jack." He replied. As we talked I soon discovered he used meth. This was the worst thing that could've happened. I came to Lake Havasu to get away from meth. Next thing you know we're smokin' meth like I never left Anaheim.

Jack starts xplaining the cost of meth in the area. "A thousand dollars an ounce!" I replied, as Jack kept talking.

Instead of listening, my mind kept thinking about all the money I could make in this area. That's five hundred dollars profit for each ounce. My mind came back to reality before I cut him off, "Jack, excuse me. But I have to get home." I hated to be like that, yet Renee was probably concerned about me being gone so long. It'd been over two hours.

As Jack sent me to my house, which was right around the corner, I got his phone number, explaining I would call him later.

When I returned home, Renee and I unpacked our belongings. Everything seemed so different. The house had three bedrooms (one master) and two bathrooms. The living room was connected to the kitchen. The house was brand new and really nice. The garage was also connected to the kitchen. I couldn't get over how pitch black it was outside at night, but I'd get used to it.

The next morning, I was woke up to Cory crying in his bedroom next to ours. Light was barely shining through the curtains. As soon as I picked him up out of his crib, he stopped crying. Cory knew he was about to be fed. I headed to the kitchen to grab his bottle. When he finished eating I would take him for a ride on the go-kart. He'd love it.

After I fed him I put him in bed with Renee and went to eat myself. I smoked about a quarter gram of meth, ate two bowls of Marshmallow Rice Crispy cereal, then lit a smoke. As I looked over at the go-kart Cory waddled out into the garage smiling at me."Are you ready to go bye, bye?"

Cory tried to say something but still couldn't talk yet. He knew what bye, bye meant though.

I opened the garage so I could warm up the go-kart. Cory started to get excited, knowing that he was going for a ride.

"Hold on little buddy." I told him as he came towards the idling go-kart.

I picked Cory up sat in the go-kart, and placed him on my lap. Then slowly hit the gas.

As I drove down the street there was no traffic. I slowly made my way around the block to see what I was dealing with traffic-wise. It was clear just like the blue sky. So I gave the go-kart more gas, and Cory laughed harder. Cory was all smiles until we pulled into the driveway, skidding to a stop right in front of Renee.

"Be careful, dumb-ass!" Renee yelled.

I handed Cory to Renee and turned the cart around and punched the gas. I wanted to race around the block a few times. As I got to the middle of the driveway there was a loud boom! The motor died. A hole was blown through the motor, spraying motor oil all over Rich's new driveway.

My heart sank to my stomach. I have the worst luck. grabbed a bristle brush and started scrubbing Rich's new driveway with every kind of solvent and cleaner I could find. I must've scrubbed for hours, with no luck in removing all the oil. I was bummed out!

As my meth supply got lower I decided to make a call. Jack had money to buy meth and I had places to score it in Anaheim. So it was on. Against Renee's pleas for me not to go back to Anaheim, I went anyways. I had Jack drive me to a U-Haul rental and rented another van. They were great for running dope. Most importantly, they were never suspected by the cops late at night. Plus, you can disconnect the speedometer, stopping it from registering miles, meaning you would pay for less mileage.

I explained to Renee that I would be back in a few days.

With tears in her eyes, I left. I sped to Desert Center to fill up on gas and headed to Orange County.

I felt guilty leaving Renee and Cory, but I would be back. Plus, I needed to see Anaheim for a while. I felt a little homesick like I was missing something. I thought leaving Anaheim would be easy, I was wrong. The streets were calling me back.

I headed straight toward Kristle's mom's apartment. There I discovered that Chucky got busted a few days earlier and was now serving one year at Chuckwalla State Prison in Blyth.

I couldn't believe it. The first thing I did was mail him a $500 money order to help him out. Kristle decided to go back and finish high school, so I was on my own again. I was going back to Arizona anyways soon as I scored some meth for Jack. With my 22 Beretta in my pocket I headed to Westminster to see Tony. I met a guy named Cisco who had just been released from prison. Cisco been hanging around whiteboys for years. He's not your typical Mexican. It didn't take long for me to realize we'd get along great. And together we hit the streets, like Chucky and me.

Cisco and I came up on two stolen Suzuki GSXR-750's and rode them all over the County, running amuck until the next morning. When I decided that we should go see Vinnie in West Anaheim. Together we raced down Beach Blvd. towards the 91 freeway. It was early in the morning, meaning traffic would be bumper to bumper. Luckily, we were riding motorcycles, because traffic would only get worse.

When we rode up the 91 freeway on ramp, we slowed to maneuver through traffic. Soon as Cisco and I made it to the fast lane, I went full throttle speeding through cars. A couple cars honked their horns as if that would slow me down. My speedometer was broken so no idea how fast I was going.

We headed to Vinnie's pad. I met Vinnie through Emily. Vinnie was in his 40's, a lot older than I. He didn't run the streets like most, just stayed home and kept out of trouble.

Cisco and I hung around Vinnie's pad smoking meth. While we were getting high, I heard Vinnie mention that Cody died in a high speed chase with the Anaheim Police the day before. I thought, *I was just talking to him the other day.* Cisco and I finished getting high and went our separate ways.

Without Chucky it was hard to locate a good deal on meth. His connection had disappeared. I headed for Tony's pad to burn some time. I'd ask around at his pad if anyone knew where to score meth.

Over the next several months so many things happened. Renee moved back to Orange County, to La Habra, with her sister Rachelle. Renee was pregnant with our child. I just couldn't get away from the streets, like I was attached. I wanted to be there for Renee but I was so messed up on drugs that they were the only thing I could think about.

Rachelle is younger than Renee with blonde hair. Her boyfriend was in prison for selling meth. I never met him though. I came and went from Rachelle's apartment like I lived there.

Drugs had ruled my life for so many years that I didn'tknow anything different. Now I was a full blown criminal with a mentality that was unpredictable and dangerous.

Cisco and I did whatever we wanted to earn money, for drugs, and anything else we wanted. I had no idea who I was anymore, but then again, I never did.

During Renee's pregnancy, I was amazed I made it through. Homeboys came and went like the seasons, in and out of jail or prison. I felt I was just waiting for my time to be locked-up or even killed. Every day was a struggle to trust anyone.

When I wasn't with Cisco, I was at my safe house, Kristle's mom's. Where I could eat, sleep and be with the only family I felt I had. Trusting certain people had always been a problem for me since running the streets in the early 90s. Rio Vista and Lincoln in East Anaheim, taught me a lot of hard lessons.

One day at Kristle's her uncle Jason had just paroled. He's a member of CWB (Crazy Whiteboy's) like Matt. I became part of the same gang. Jason asked me if I wanted to be a crazy white boy, and I said yes. Now I was a gang member. Jason never stayed out of prison for long. He'd always show up fresh out of prison healthy, only to lose all that weight he gained using meth.

One night Jason and I bought this Tech-22 for a little meth from this tweeker. I wanted to make it into an automatic. So Jason and I took it apart and filed down the pirate mechanism, and headed for the nearest freeway to test it.

As we're driving down the freeway at 2 in the morning, I looked around to make sure no one was around. Cars in front would not hear the shots, so I didn't trip on those cars. I always shot at freeway signs. Why? I don't know; I just did.

When the coast was clear I told Jason to hold the steering wheel as I chambered a round and fired up into the night sky. I heard POP! POP! And it jammed after firing two rounds. As I pulled the gun back through window into the car, it fired another round shattering the front windshield.

"Chris, your fuckin' crazy!" Jason yelled as I pulled the car over and parked on the side of the freeway.

"Come on Dawg. Let's get out of here before the cops come." I replied as I grabbed all my belongings out of the car.

A few days later I met this girl named Alyssa at Tony's pad. Alyssa was around thirty years old with blond hair and blue eyes. In no time at all we were talking away in Tony's garage smokin' meth. That's when I discovered she did the check scam to make money.

In the early 90s the check scam was popular on the streets with tweekers. People who stole cars would find checks, IDs, etc, and then would sell them to people like Alyssa, who would use these checks to buy food, clothes, and things of that nature. Next thing I know we're driving down Beach Blvd., in Alyssa's VW Bug, just enjoying the day hoping to come up on some new clothes by the end of the day. We stopped by a few places to purchase some odds and ends. Alyssa explained to me that she needed to stop by her friend's pad off Ball Road and Euclid to bring her some food.

Since returning from Lake Havasu, so many things had happened. Because of me shooting at Aron, and supposedly

Chucky and laughing at Cody being killed in the police chase. There was several people spreading rumors that their buddies were going to jump us, or worse.

Kristle called me one day explaining that Josh and his friends were looking for me. Meaning to me that they wanted to kill me, beat me up, or even rob me. Either way, I could care less.

"Chris, I warned them. I told them you're way too smart to be caught slipping, and that you would shoot them."

As Kristle said all this to me, I just paused on the other end of the line, then replied, "Kristle, you tell them I'll be around doing the same thing, and good luck!"

When Alyssa and I arrived at her friend's apartment, she explained to me to wait in the car, and that she would be right back.

"No problem." I replied. I adjusted the review mirror so I could see behind me.

The complex was two stories and considering the area it was kept nice. Houses were on one side of the street, and apartments on the other. People were going about their daily activities as I waited patiently.

In the car's review mirror I noticed several hinky looking tweekers, which gave me a bad feeling. They were actually looking my way, but I brushed it off. I had my gun, so I was not worried.

Several minutes later Alyssa appears on the balcony, overlooking Webster St., and waves for me to come inside.

*Alright.* I thought to myself, as I headed toward the entrance to the complex. Alyssa was waiting at the top of the stairs with a big smile.

As I followed Alyssa to the apartment, I looked around for those people I'd seen earlier hanging out front and didn't notice anyone. I followed Alyssa inside with my hand on my gun.

As I sat on the couch with Alyssa, I felt a little at ease. The apartment was actually nice. A few young kids were running around (one stopped giving me a, who are you look) then kept playing.

Alyssa stood up to go talk to her friend in the kitchen, leaving me on the couch. Not a second later those guys hanging out front of the apartment walked through the front door staring at me. Right away I knew something was up.

These guys went into the kitchen, mumbled something to Alyssa's friend, then left the apartment without another word. From my experience it was time for me to leave before they returned with more friends, or who knows what else. I knew I wasn't trippin'.

I walked into the kitchen and told Alyssa, "We're leaving!"

That's when this guy appeared from one of the back bedrooms explaining to me, "Hey, these guys are saying you clowned their friend Cody that was killed in a high speed chase with the police. And that they're going to get you when you leave."

I paused for a second as I stared at this big-ass white boy all tattooed up, and replied, "I didn't come here to disrespect your pad. But if those lames try to harm me, I will shoot them."

I grabbed Alyssa by the hand and we left the apartment. When we got at the stairs leading down to the car several guys were standing at the bottom waiting for me.

It was starting to get dark at this time. "Alyssa, go start your car and wait for me. They won't harm you." Alyssa looked at me confused, not sure what she should do. Then started down the stairs.

They let Alyssa go to her car like I knew they would. I was ten feet behind Alyssa with my hand in my pocket ready to pull my 22 Beretta. Thinking that it was going to get ugly soon. As I stood at the bottom of the stairs surrounded by these guys, ready for whatever, I quickly realized these lames weren't going to do shit.

"Figures." I muttered as I walked to Alyssa's car.

When I hopped in the passenger's seat I looked to my right, noticing these guys coming towards the car. I pulled out my gun, holding it in view. Then these idiots start trying to punch me through the window. I've got my right hand blocking their punches, all the while holding my gun in my left hand. Then I hear the door click as one of them starts to pull open the door.

With a pocket full of money, and dope, and not knowing their real intentions, I lifted my left hand and pointed my gun through the window and fired away. POP! POP! POP!

Alyssa started to scream, "They're shooting at us!" As the car lurched forward and stalled out.

"Alyssa, get in the passenger's seat!" I replied.

When I opened the car door, I only saw one guy, crawling away in a trail of blood. I walked up and knelt down and said, "You stupid fucker! You know I carry a gun."

As I made my way around the car to get in the driver's seat, I noticed people everywhere looking at me. "Fuck, I'm done." I whispered to myself as I got into the car and sped down Webster ST., hoping to at least get away before the cops arrived. I made a left turn on Ball Rd., then a right at the next light.

As we raced away from the scene all these thoughts ran through my mind. My biggest concern was Renee being pregnant and our baby being due in a couple of months. My chances of getting away with this crime didn't look good.

At that moment I decided to head to Tony's pad. While explaining to Alyssa that she better paint her car before driving anywhere else, The cops would be looking for her white VW Bug, without a doubt.

I also told her if she got busted before me to tell the cops exactly what happened. I knew she had children, and I didn't want this to be the reason she lost them or went to jail or prison on my behalf.

Alyssa agreed with everything I had said, handling the whole situation really well.

Soon as we arrived at Tony's pad we put her car in his garage so it would be out of sight. I sat silently in her car smoking meth for a least an hour. As I realized how much trouble I was actually in, my pager started to vibrate.

When I looked at the screen to see who was calling me there was no code to identify the caller. As I sat there trying to figure out who the caller could be I decided I had nothing to lose and called the number. On the second ring I heard, "Hello, is this Chris?"

"Yeah."

"Chris Curtis?"

"Yeah, it's me!" I replied getting irritated. "This is the Anaheim Police Department; don't you think you should come turn yourself in?"

I sat there unable to speak, thinking, *Son of a Bitch! Is this really happening?* Then replied, "For what?"

"You know why." The unknown officer replied.

That's when I hung up the phone knowing I was going to prison, and for a long time, if not forever.

Not ten minutes later Cisco called me, "You crazy mother fucker!"

I'm thinking to myself, "How does he know already."

"Are you there Chris?"

"Yeah, I'm still here."

Cisco went on to explain how he knew what had happened. Cisco was down the street at his brother's apartment. When that tattooed guy at Alyssa's friend's apartment went and told Cisco everything that had happened.

"They're saying you shot two people. You know that right?" Cisco added, "And one guy died."

You could hear a pin drop it was so quiet. Cisco broke the silence, "Just Kiddin' fool!" And started laughing. "Fuck them lames, Cisco. You know the cops already paged me? Saying that I should turn myself in."

"Already!" Cisco replied shocked. Cisco said to stay put, he was coming to pick me up.

When I hung up I thought about the best way to avoid being caught by the cops. Realizing a fast motorcycle would do the trick and with a possible life sentence over my head, I decided to run like my life depended on it. I'd either get away or die trying in the process.

As I sat in Tony's garage, I called my old friend Michele. She'd definitely freak out hearing this news.

Outside I heard a car approaching with a loud stereo.

Realizing Cisco was pulling into the driveway I put away all my belongings. A second later Cisco opened the garage, knowing I was there, and said, "Let's split homie, and grab something to eat. You look starved." I picked up my backpack and replied, "I am dawg. Like you wouldn't believe."

# CHAPTER 10

As I stepped out of Cisco's car in front of Michele's pad, I realized how loyal Cisco was. It's crazy too. He's dangerous, doesn't hesitate to commit a crime. But the more I hung out with him, the more I trusted him. I knew he had my back.

"Cisco, don't tell anyone about this place."

Cisco turned up his radio and gave me a look that said, "Really fool!" I just smiled as he drove off in his gangster looking ride.

Michele stood at the front door as I walked up the front path. I could see the concern in her eyes. "Chris, you've gotta leave the state."

"And go where?" I replied looking around the house.

The house was empty. You could clearly see they had just moved in. No furniture or pictures on the walls.

"Mother fucken' Chris Curtis! You really did it this time, didn't you?" Gerrid yelled, coming out of the back room. Gerrid was Michele's boyfriend. We've had our problems, but for the most part, we're cool. Gerrid's about six feet tall and could smoke meth with the best of them.

I looked up and replied, "I guess I did. Michele, can you take me to my mom's? I better go visit her before I do anything else."

Michele explained to me that she would take me in a little while. As I waited, I sat on the carpet with my back against the wall staring at the front door. I listened to Gerrid's police scanner with my gun in my lap. I knew the coming days would be tough."

Hours later I woke up to Gerrid kicking my leg, "Wake up Chris! Your pager is beeping." I fell asleep against the wall. I looked down for my gun and it was gone. Before I could ask Gerrid reached inside his pocket, "Here's your gun. You might wanna throw in a lake or something and get a new one. I'm sure the cops will be looking for it."

I reached in my pocket for my meth so I could wake up. As I was smoking meth I scrolled through my pager to see who had been calling. Kristle had called ten times alone, along with an unknown number, who ended up being the cops again. "Like I'll call them back." I mumbled to myself.

Kristle answered on the second ring, "Christopher Curtis, you're crazy."

I just laughed and replied, "You know, I've been hearing that a lot in the last 24 hours."

The line was chucky for a couple of seconds before Kristle said, "I warned them Chris. Summer called and explained the whole thing to me."

"Did Summer tell you that the cops called me on my pager an hour later?"

"No, Chris. She didn't tell me that." Kristle paused for a second then said, "guess you're going to prison."

I changed the subject. "Tell Chucky what happened when he calls. I'm sure he'll get a laugh out of this shit. Also, Kristle, the cops will have a tough time catching me."

"Chris, don't do anything stupid!"

"Kristle, do I ever do anything stupid?"

When we finished talking I went to look for Michele only to realize she had left. I had to figure out what I was going to do. Now that it was getting dark outside I felt more comfortable leaving the house. I noticed Pat had a GSXR 750 in the backyard. I figured I would talk him out of the motorcycle. Maybe he'd let me borrow it for a couple days. Which with our history, might be tough.

"Gerrid!" I yelled from the backyard. I needed this motorcycle.

"What do you want Chris?" Gerrid replied as he walked through the screen door leading into the backyard. I got straight to the point, "Need to borrow this motorcycle for a few days."

Gerrid looked down at the bike in deep thought. I thought for sure he'd say no. Then he looks up at me, "You know it's stolen, right?"

I laughed and replied, "Do you actually think I give a crap? Where's a helmet for this bike?"

With a helmet on my head, gun in my pocket, I was on my way. I said to myself, *You'll never see this motorcycle again.* Now you know why Gerrid and I didn't get along.

I headed down Orange towards the 57 freeway. I had to go see Renee at her sister's. She was not going to be happy about this whole situation. When we found out that she was pregnant, I promised when our baby was born I would stop running the streets. Now I might go to prison for the rest of my life, and that's if I didn't die running.

When I finished explaining the whole incident to Renee, she looked away disgusted and hurt. I couldn't blame her. Cory was on the couch asleep next to her. I didn't go looking for these guys. They came after me because of some dumb rumor and got shot in the process. They knew I carried a gun with me at all times. And certainly knew I would use it if I had to.

I left late that night heading towards Westminster, wondering if I would ever see Renee or Cory again.

It was the weirdest feeling not knowing what would happen. As I sped down the 57 freeway toward the 91 freeway, I knew my life would never be the same.

Over the next couple of weeks Cisco and I survived doing whatever we needed to get by. Cisco had a PAL Warrant

(Parole At Large), and I was wanted for two counts of attempted murder. With both of us considered armed and dangerous, who knew what would happen.

When I pulled into Tony's driveway, Cisco and Billy were leaning against Billy's El Camino talking. Billy's El Camino was white and looked worn out, yet it still ran good and was registered and totally legal. I was fairly new to this clique of friends but became close to Cisco and Billy fast. We all had the same mentality. Smoke meth and make money any way possible.

As I walked in removing my helmet Billy reached out to shake my hand, "What's up?" He said with a smile.

"Oh, you know. Smoken' speed!"

Cisco laughed, "Fuckin' Chris. Let's go inside."

When Cisco opened Tony's garage I noticed several cans of spray paint laying around the garage floor. Alyssa's VW Bug was now primer gray. I was actually shocked she listened to my suggestion. I opened her car door to search for empty shell casings from the shooting. I found four and put them in my pocket as I sat on the couch. Billy asked, "Let me borrow your motorcycle Chris?"

"You know its stolen, right?" I replied.

"So What!" Billy cried as he tossed me the keys to his El Camino. Then gets real serious, "Chris, please don't shoot anyone in my car. I'm on parole and don't want my ride burnt." What he meant was if a car had been used for a robbery, or shooting, etc, it's burnt like a hot gun, but really hard to get rid of.

As I passed Billy the pipe full of meth, I said, "You know I smoke a lot of meth, right?"

"Fucken Chris. I'm serious homeboy" Billy replied as he blew a big cloud of smoke. Cisco and I look at each other and busted up laughing.

"Real funny." Billy said as he walked inside Tony's apartment. I could tell Billy was trying to do good and get off parole. Yet with friends like us that was highly unlikely.

When I left Tony's in Billy's El Camino I made a left onto

Beach Blvd. Suddenly remembering about Jack in Lake Havasu. It'd been several months since leaving for Anaheim to score meth with his money. As I drove under the 22 freeway I said to myself, "Chris , you're a dirt bag." It's so easy to lose yourself in the streets.

I should've never left Lake Havasu. My chances of living a normal life had been ruined. I always said I would never be like my dad, and now I'd probably be spending the rest of my life in prison, leaving my unborn child without a dad. I shook those thoughts out of my head as I turned onto the 91 freeway, heading towards East Anaheim.

As the weeks passed, so did what little faith I had of staying out of prison. Friends were asking me not to come around anymore, in fear of what could happen if the cops found me at their house. Cops always made life difficult for anyone involved with hiding wanted felons. Especially if kids were involved. I felt betrayed by a lot of people.

Renee and Rachelle had moved to an apartment off Rio Vista and Lincoln, in Anaheim. Right in the middle of my old neighborhood where I started running the streets.

The complex was in excellent condition. With an upstairs and downstairs. Two bedrooms up top, with a bathroom, and a nice living room that connected to a kitchen. Plus, it had a small backyard. Walking through the complex you'd forget you were in Anaheim, seeing the nice green grass, and rose bushes scattered all around. I was happy they moved here. La Habra was too far. Our child would be born in a few weeks, and I planned on visiting as much as possible.

Billy was taking care of this guy's house who lived in Diamond Bar, off the 57 freeway. This house was big and surrounded by an excellent neighborhood. Nobody knew the location except a chosen few, which made it a great safe house for me. I could drive out to Diamond Bar and go to sleep without worrying about waking up with a gun in my face or worse.

One time I was drving home in Billy's El Camino and just exited the 57 freeway. Sure enough an L.A. County Police car gets on my tail. Billy's El Camnino had bad tags, but it was recently registered with proof in the back window. But cops will be cops, and he hit his lights, pulling me over. "Son of a bitch," I mumbled to myself.

I start going thru all these scenarios, do I have drugs in my pocket, my gun was duct tapped under the hood, and figured that I was cool. "Can I see your license and registration sir." The cop asked.

The day before Billy's girlfriend handed me this California driver's license she stole out of a car. "Hey, Chris." She says to me as she hands me this ID, "This guy looks like you." I grabbed the ID, gave a quick look and replied, "Sure does!" And put it in my wallet.

I handed this cop that ID and started running down this story to him, "Officer, this is my buddy's car. My truck broke down and I was late for work, so I took his car."

He looked at me and my dirty clothes and said "Wait here sir I'll be right back." When the cop walked to his car I lit a smoke thinking it would be my last for a while. I thought for sure I was going to jail.

I looked across the street at the gas station and saw Billy's girlfriend and her friend looking at me. You could see the sad expression on their faces. I just looked down and shook my head. I would've ran, but I gave Billy my word that I wouldn't harm his car.

When I looked back I saw the cop approaching the El Camino. I held my breath thinking about what could happen. I was shocked by what he said, "You have a nice day." As he handed me my ID back. I couldn't believe it. My hands were shaking when I lit another smoke and drove off. I pulled into the driveway behind Billy's girlfriend, "Chris, you're so lucky! I thought for sure you were going to jail." I pulled at that ID she gave me and replied, "Me too. Let's go smoke some meth."

"Chris, you're a trip." She replied as we walked into the pad.

A few days later I received a call from Renee, "Chris, I'm going to the hospital to have our baby. Please meet me there!"

"Okay, Don't trip!" I replied. I wasn't about to miss my baby being born. I'd already be missing years of my child's life being stuck in prison. Which I couldn't stand the thought of.

Anaheim Memorial was down by Euclid Ave. I called my mom so she could meet us there. The whole time I kept wondering if the cops would be waiting for me at the hospital. But it wasn't about to stop me, even if the cops were there.

When I arrived at the hospital so many people were waiting. Rachelle, Renee's best friend Ann, my mom, my brother Jay, and several other people I didn't know. Right away this heavy-set nurse rushed me into this smock. Renee had already been prepped for a C-section. I didn't know what to expect, let alone know what to do. The whole process seemed to go so fast. Then that nurse rushed me into a room with Renee. She looked so scared with tears in her eyes. Right away she grabbed my hand, squeezing it like never before.

"Don't worry Renee! It'll be okay!" I said. I walked by her gurney as they wheeled her into this big room with all this medical equipment. Renee had already received an epidural to numb her from the waist down. I thought my hand would break from her squeezing it, and they hadn't even cut her stomach yet.

The doctor walked in and rubbed red iodine all over her stomach, and cut down her stomach. Then he used some stick to cauterize the blood vessels. After that he used a metal hook-looking instrument to help him pull out our baby girl. I started feeling tears roll down my cheeks. It was the strangest feeling becoming a dad, and the thought of missing her grow up while I was in prison hurt like hell. I held my daughter Brooke for a while, before they took her to the nursery.

Ann saw me come out of Renee's hospital room and said, "Look at Chris, with tears in his eyes." She said playfully. We both walked together to go see Brooke in the hospital nursery. I had so many emotions running through me that I'd never felt before. It was a trip!

As I was leaving the hospital, I passed a chapel. I thought I better ask God to give me a chance to raise Brooke, so I opened the door and went inside. I felt at ease walking down the aisle of the church. A big cross stood at the front of a big stained-glass window. I was all alone in the church. I knelt and prayed, "God please give me another chance to be with my daughter. If you do I promise I'll never get in trouble again. And if I do, give me a life sentence because I deserve it."

I stood up, looking at the cross one more time and was out the door. When I got outside I scanned the parking lot for signs of any cops. And was shocked not to find any waiting for me. I drove out of the parking lot relieved that everything went well.

As I drove down Euclid St. I lit a smoke. I felt lost inside. Almost every pad I've been to had been raided by the police looking for me. I started trippin' on all my friends. I couldn't trust anyone at this point. It came to a point where I didn't stay more than 20 minutes at a pad before leaving. I always had this uneasy feeling that I was being watched or something. I even remember saying to myself, *can't wait till this is over. Whatever the outcome.*

Michele called from Renee's a couple of days after Brooke was born. "Chris, Brooke looks just like you!" I smiled and couldn't help but feel proud. I asked Michele to wait for me; I was on my way over.

When I drove into the neighborhood, I noticed an Anaheim Police cruiser right before I turned into Renee's neighborhood, which made me suspicious, yet I just told myself that I was trippin'.

I parked Billy's El Camino as close to Renee's apartment as possible.

When I strolled into the apartment, I saw Michele holding Brooke with a big smile. I sat next to Michele so I could get a good look at my daughter. "Poor girl does look like me, Michele." I said.

"Chris, you have to get out of this state," Michele cried, "Before they catch you!"

"Where would I go?" I asked. "Lake Havasu is out of the question."

I stood up and headed upstairs to talk to Renee before I left.

I didn't like the feeling I was getting being at the apartment. As I arrived at the top of the stairs Renee was coming out of the bathroom with a towel wrapped around her head.

"Renee!" I mumbled knowing she was upset with me. I promised not to leave her alone to raise Cory and Brooke, which is exactly what could happen.

"Chris, turn yourself in before you get into more trouble," Renee begged as she sat on her bed.

"Renee, you know I could never do that." I wanted to tell her that I'll probably end up with life in prison if I turned myself in. But I couldn't upset her anymore.

"Look Renee, I'll be back later. I have to return Billy's El Camino and get Gerrid's motorcycle back to him; then I'll come back so we can talk."

I gave her a quick kiss and headed down the stairs. I said goodbye to Michele, and Brooke. And was out the front door, wondering if I would ever make it back.

Billy had broken the chain on the Suzuki GSXR-750 motorcycle, trying to do wheelies, and it was now parked at some tweeker pad off Dale Ave., where Daryl was staying.

Daryl is another tweeker I met through Billy and Cisco. I didn't know him well. I still had to replace the chain on the motorcycle, so I could return it to Pat. This same house was raided by the police looking for me, only six days before. I didn't even wanna be near this pad, but I had no choice.

As I drove Lincoln Ave. towards Dale Ave., my pager went nuts. Renee had paged me six times in a row. So I pulled over to a payphone. I thought something might be wrong with Brooke. I dialed the number, and it didn't even ring all the way through one time before Renee picked up, "CHRIS!"

"Yeah, Renee. What's up?"

"Right after you left the Anaheim Police showed up looking for you. They raided the apartment."

I sat chucky for a few seconds thinking to myself, *Son of a bitch!* "What did they say?"

"They asked if you were there and if you would shoot at them when they found you. Turn yourself in Chris!" Renee cried.

I didn't know what to say. I lit a smoke and replied, "I'll be back there later tonight. The cops won't expect me to come back so early. I love you and I'll see you later."

As I was hanging up the phone I heard Renee saying something, but I didn't wanna hear it. I tossed my smoke, lit a fresh one and drove out of the parking lot.

I drove down the street in silence. There was no doubt that the cops were serious. I'd either be in prison soon, or dead from running.

As I parked in front of Daryl's I threw my smoke out the window. I sat in the car looking in all three mirrors to see if I could see anyone sitting in their cars. My instincts were telling me not to be at this house, so I duck-taped my gun under the hood of the car and walked up the driveway.

Daryl was waiting for me in the garage, "Hey Chris. How's it goin?" Daryl asked.

"You know, same o shit," I muttered, "Where's the tools and the chain for the motorcycle?"

"Right next to the bike," Daryl said.

"I have to get this chain on the bike and get the fuck out of here. This pad makes me uncomfortable." I replied.

"Well, because of you Chris, every pad has been raided." Daryl added.

"Yeah, I know. Alyssa was busted a few days ago in her VW Bug, huh?"

"Yeah." Daryl whispered, "I'll be right back. I have to go get my dope."

As Daryl walked off I got to work on the motorcycle. Billy didn't know how to replace a chain on a motorcycle, so here I was, a sitting duck in the garage. Hopefully, this whole process shouldn't take me long.

I'd been dodging the Anaheim Police for weeks. My hopes were always that I would be on a motorcycle when they surrounded me. I'd have such a better chance of escaping. One second the police would be behind me, the next I would be gone.

The Helipad for the Anaheim Police department was directly across the street from a tow yard I used to hang out at while living with Dina. Also, Dina's house was close enough to hear the Police Helicopter lifting off from the helipad. When I was bored at Dina's I would grab the police scanner and listen to it. I'd hear patrol cars being called for assistance. Then I'd hear the helicopter take off.

If you get into a high speed chase with the police you have about 3-5 minutes to ditch them and your ride too. Then you have to run like hell. If you're unlucky the helicopter is already in the air, patrolling the city. If that's the case, you're pretty much busted.

As I was replacing the chain on Gerrid's motorcycle it was a warm afternoon in the middle of the week. Since parking Billy's El Camino in front of Daryl's pad I felt like something was wrong. I had the chain and safety clip off within five minutes. Now I just had to tighten the wheel, bleed the clutch, and tighten the gear shifter.

All of a sudden my instincts were telling me to get the hell out of there. It was like I could see the cops coming to bust me. My heart started thumping in my chest. Quickly I made sure the tension on the chain was okay and tightened the gear shifter as best as I could. I knew the cops were coming. I put my helmet on and pushed the motorcycle out of the garage and down the driveway. I didn't even take time to bleed the clutch. At the bottom of the riveway I jumped on the motorcycle and put it in first gear, hitting the starter button. The motorcycle sputtered to life. When I pulled onto Dale Ave, police cars were coming from both directions.

I sped past the first unmarked car at sixty miles per hour at least. Then made my first right onto Orangewood, going towards Disneyland. I was going 100 miles per hour in seconds. Flying through a stop sign, barely missing a car. I looked back to see if any cops were behind me, which they weren't. I slowed down to make a left hand turn. Soon as I turned the corner the gear came off the gear box. Quickly I pulled over to the side of the road. As soon as the motorcycle stalled out I heard the Thump! Thump! Thump! The police helicopter was already circling above me. That helicopter had to be waiting for me at that house.

As I tightened the gear shifter, I heard several police sirens getting closer to me. When I stood up I could easily see cops speeding toward me now. I jumped back on the motorcycle, hit the starter button and flew up onto the sidewalk to avoid all of the cop cars, and once again sped through traffic.

I lost the cop cars again with ease, but the helicopter was still up in the air. At speeds of over 100 mph, I was running red lights with no fear at all. I heard cars honking as I flew through several iersections. My adrenaline was so high I couldn't think straight. I made a left turn into a residential neighborhood and was up to 90 mph in seconds. All of a sudden I saw a crossing guard holding a red stop sign. The first thing I thought was kids and I had no clutch to down shift, so I swerved, barely missing the crossing guards. After that I lost all train of thought and with a cull-d-sac approaching, I could go left or crash into the house at the end. So, I hit the brakes a little too hard and that sent me into the concrete, doing a Pete Rose across the pavement.

My arms felt like they were on fire as I slid across Embassy Circle with my motorcycle right in front of me, the whole length of the cul-de-sac. The motorcycle hit the curb, only to flip over onto someone's front lawn. I jumped to my feet and ran, jumping fences, as fast as I could.

I ended up on West Lincoln Ave., in an office complex. I ran up a stairway, kicked down a door, and went inside, shutting the door behind me. I ended up inside a janitor's closet, which was the size of a bathroom. With the helicopter circling above me I knew I was busted. So, I lit a smoke and waited. It was finally over.

All I heard was cops yelling, "Up here!" With footsteps pounding up the stairway. They knew right where I was located. Police helicopters have heat sensors that detect body heat. I just wanted to finish my smoke before they kicked down the door.

There was a big chance this could all go really bad for me. They could easily blow me away coming through the door. Boom! The door came flying open, along with several guns pointed at me. My hands went up in the air with a cigarette hanging out of my mouth.

"Get face down on the ground, now!" And all that drama you see in the movies. I was surprised that they didn't shoot me. They cuffed me, stood me up, and walked me down the stairs. Two detectives approached me and said, "We've been looking all over for you. You should've turned yourself in. Those guys you shot said they started the whole thing."

I just ignored them. Then the funniest thing happened. A patrol officer who used to patrol Dina's neighborhood walked up to me and said, "Hey Jay. You're going to prison Huh?" Those two detectives looked over, "Jay! His name is Chris Curtis."

That patrol officer used to stop me all the time. I would give him my brother's name because I usually had warrants for my arrest. That cop looked at me and said, "You're good." And walked off. I couldn't help but smile.

They put me inside an ambulance. Blood was all over me. My arms literally felt like they were on fire.

When we arrived at the hospital, they handcuffed me to a bed. Then scrubbed my arms with a hard brush to remove all of the dirt from the pavement, including rocks and whatever else I picked up during my slide across the pavement. Talk about pain. The RN wouldn't even give me any pain medication because I was in police custody. Soon as they finished cleaning my wounds my arms were wrapped in bandages, and I was transported to the Anaheim Police Station.

The next morning they woke me up to interrogate me. They wanted to ask me all about the shooting. Before they could ask me a question, I said, "I want a lawyer." They escorted me right back to my cell, where I went right back to sleep.

The next day I was transferred to O.C.J. (Orange County Jail). Better known as the main jail. Going through booking was terrible. The whole process takes 24 hours. For us who visit the jail, we call it going through the Loop.

Soon as you walk through the door your first stop is medical. The nurses ask you questions required by the law. Have you ever attempted suicide, do you have any mental health problems, and are you hurt? After that they strip search you and place you in one of twenty tanks. These tanks are filled with drunks, gangsters, and weirdos.

Then they switch you from one tank to another slowly making your way through the loop. You get fingerprinted, and sent to classification, where they ask you more questions. Before they place a colored wristband around your wrist, Red is for High power, Orange for gang affiliation, Violence, Etc., Yellow if you've been to prison, White if you haven't, and Blue for Protective Custody.

I was given a white band.

After you've been classified, they place you in a tank full of inmates. Then they shower you and you'll wait several hours to receive your bed roll. Which includes a mattress, blanket & sheets. Before they send you to your cell they search and harass you some more. Then escort you upstairs.

Cisco was already on the third floor. They arrested him a few days before me. Gerrid, Michele's boyfriend was downstairs from me. I guess Gerrid was arrested while I was at the police station for manufacturing meth. I was charged with two counts of attempted Murder, along with Felony evading the police.

The two guys I shot of course had friends inside of the jail. It always happens like that. Everyone has their own crew. O.C.J. is full of drama. First, they said I shot them in the back. Their friends tried everything they could to put me in the wrong, but it didn't work. I had friends too. Luckily the drama didn't last long.

On my first court date, I brought back the police report. It simply read that I shot one guy in the chest and one in the lower back. Probably because he turned and ran. I can't call back the bullets. They both lived. Those idiots came to a gunfight without a gun and were shot. Besides that, they all ratted on me, except the guy with all those tattoos, who warned me not to leave.

Michele came to visit me the day after I arrived at the jail. I looked like I'd been in a fight with the asphalt. Bandages up and down my arms. She also brought Renee, Cory, and Brooke. Poor Brooke did look like me. All our friends called her Crib-Curtis. Which always made me smile.

Brooke was born on Dec 28, 1995. I ended up in the county jail at the beginning of February 1996. Renee was mad, as she had every right to be. Cory cried every time he came to visit because he couldn't get through the glass. I felt guiltier and guiltier every time.

I talked to my mom a few days after arriving at the county jail. Mom knew this day was coming long before it happened. Michele took me to see my mom after the shooting. I explained what happened. She was in denial right away. "Chris, are you sure they knew it was you?"

"Mom, the cops paged me after the shooting!" The whole time I'm telling her this I'm thinking, *I should've shot your boyfriend years ago.* As I'm looking at him sitting on the couch. Mom said, "I like it better when you're in jail. At least I know you're safe."

On February 27, 1996, I went to court. My Public Defender walked up, "Mr. Curtis. They've dropped the two counts of Attempted Murder to two counts of Aggravated Assault with firearm. And they're offering you six years, with two strikes, at 85%." I signed that deal so fast. I was off to prison 30 days after signing.

# CHAPTER 11

As we drove up to Delano State Prison, I was surprised by the size of their reception center. I knew then prison would be totally different than the county jail. I was the 5th inmate on the bus. The Correctional Officer made an example out of the 6th inmate. This inmate decided to talk to his homeboy as he stepped off the bus. So, the sergeant grabbed him by his jumpsuit, laid him down still shackled on the steps of the bus, and used him as a doormat. Walking on and off the bus several times stepping right on top of him. No one talked after that until we reached the holding tanks.

Delano's R&R (which stands for receiving and release), is designed to receive and ship inmates out by the hundreds daily. Delano is one of many reception centers located inside California's prison system. This reception center has several buses leaving every day to fill the state's prisons. Holding tanks are around the outer edges inside R&R. The center is one big, enclosed desk, where twenty highly paid C/Os are watching monitors.

Another Sergeant lined us up for our introduction,

"Gentleman, let me be perfectly clear. Don't disrespect me or my officers, and we won't disrespect you. Follow our instructions so we can process you as fast as possible. When your name is called approach the desk with your hands behind your back. You'll have your picture taken for your ID, and you'll be fingerprinted. If everything runs smoothly, we'll give you your property. All personal clothing will be sent home or donated if you don't have money to pay for shipping. At this time, we'll remove your waist chains. You'll be stripped, searched, and walked through the metal detector. Soon as this process is completed, you receive a sack lunch."

After stuffing all 30 of us into one tank, they called us to the desk four at a time. As I approached the desk I thought to myself, *These C/O's have it made.* Practically every C/O had their own TV at their desk. The Officers asked various questions like: are you affiliated with any gangs, do you have any enemies, and what is your ethnicity?

After that they took my fingerprints for the 6th time since being arrested. Then my picture was taken, and I was finally sent to the property officer. The whole process took about a half hour. When we completed this process, we were given a bedroll containing two sheets, one pillowcase, blanket, and a fish kit. Fish kits contain: Toothbrush, soap, a few stamped envelopes, and an orientation packet explaining all the rules you must follow.

For the next few hours, I sat in the holding tank listening to everyone's stories. Whites sat with the whites, the Mexicans sat with their own, and so forth.

Finally, we were escorted to our buildings where we would housed for the next several months. Delano has 5 facilities, A, B, C, D, and a level 1 yard, which is E-facility.

They sent me to D-yard, which is cell living. Two inmates to a cell. Prison has 4 Levels with 4 being the most violent. Level 1 inmates are low risk inmates. Mostly all level 1 yards are dorm living. Which house up to 200 inmates. Level 1 yards are usually located on the outer perimeter of the prison grounds. That means no electric fence giving an inmate the opportunity to jump the fence if he wanted to. However, these low-level inmates have only months to serve. Making it unlikely to happen.

Low-level inmates are worked hard and sent home without ever really addressing the issues which sent them to prison in the first place. Violence on this 1 yard is unlikely to happen.

Level 2 yards are pretty much the same thing. Dorm living with mostly non-serious crimes. They're worked the same and released. The violence on these yards is a little worse.

Level 3 yards are mostly violent offenders, involved with gangs, working their way to Level 4 yards. The violence on these yards is much worse than both 1 & 2 combined. Correctional Officers respect you a little more on these yards too.

Level 4 yards are dangerous. You could be stabbed for walking in the wrong area of the yard, which is out of bounds for your ethnicity.

My experience started with Centinela State Prison. Because of my violent case I was sent to a level 3. When I stepped off the bus, I thought I would pass out from the heat. R&R was tiny compared to Delano's, With just 5 C/Os working the whole R&R. We received the same speech from the sergeant at Centinela. They took us inside and placed us in one of five holding tanks. Like Delano they had monitors for the C/Os to watch while processing inmates.

The process was the same: fingerprints, pictures, classification. After they processed us, they fed us sack lunches consisting of peanut butter & jelly, pack of cookies, and maybe some chips. Then after another few hours we were escorted to our new homes.

When I arrived at Centinela in June of 1996, there was 4 level 3 yards, and a level 1. I was sent to A-yard to start my term. I was a little nervous.

When you first arrive on a new yard, you're escorted directly to an orientation building. You'll stay there until you're seen by a counselor and taken to committee.

I was glad to finally be on a yard. Reception Centers are so boring. Being stuck in a little cell 23 hours a day is not cool. My homeboys from county gave me a little black & white TV, and I loved it.

Yard is usually 3 hours in the morning and 3 hours in the afternoon. They only allow one tier at a time on the yard. So upper tier goes in the morning, and lower in the afternoon. It rotates daily. Night yard runs from 7 PM to 9 PM

I had a whole different perception about prison before arriving at Centinela. For one, all that talk about people being raped isn't happening. I'm not saying it never happens, but it's rare. Matter of fact, you go to prison for raping anyone, your homeboys will try and kill you when you get off orientation. Same with child molesters and rats. Everyone is given a 128g (which inmates call paperwork), and your paperwork must be shown as soon as you arrive at prison. If you cannot produce paperwork to the other prisoners in a few days, you'll be whacked by your homeboys. It's the same with the Mexicans, but Black's politics are a little different.

My homeboy Robert was there. I knew him from Juvenile Hall. We sat around laughing about being locked up in the Youth Guidance Center. Within a few days I reccived a ducat for a job in the kitchen. Talk about being happy to work. You're able to eat all you want, and I looked starved compared to most inmates. So I ate as much as I could.

They assigned me to the split shift. Four AM to 7 AM, then 4 PM to 7 PM. After my morning shift I would meet my homeboys. It was me, Robert, Chucky, and Micky.

We'd get a slot at the weight pile on the yard, and workout for an hour. Then we'd walk the yard for a few hours. I found out quickly that level 3 yards are full of a lot of wannabe tough guys. Don't get me wrong, there are a lot of dangerous people on these yards, but not like you would think.

My first incident was with two southern Mexicans. I was on the phone in the building trying to call Renee. They both walked up to me, "Hey Wood. It's our phone time." Whiteboy's are called wood in prison. It's been like that for years.

"No it's not," I replied. "Go look at the phone list."

These two Mexicans insisted it was their phone time, so I finally said, "Okay, I'm gonna go check the list. And if my name is on that phone list I'm coming back, and you better get off."

"Okay Wood," One replied.

I walked off to go check knowing it was my phone time. I had to be sure though. Sure enough my name was on the phone list, and I got mad. This Mexican was already in a conversation when I returned. "Get off the phone!" I demanded.

He started to say something, but it was already too late. I punched him right in the face.

The cops started yelling for us to get down. "Get Down!" Over and over they yelled this at us. But I kept punching him in the face. Finally, the tower shot the block gun at us, hitting me. I stopped after that.

The block gun shoots rubber bullets, and they hurt when hit. I had a welt on my leg for days. They placed us both in handcuffs, then escorted us to the program office. This was my first 115, for fighting.

A 115 is a rule violation. Soon as I returned to my cell, my cellie was packing up all his belongings.

"Why are you packing your property?" I asked.

"Because you just beat up someone from another race without permission." He replied.

"He was trying to punk me for my phone time."

"Chris, I'm not saying you're wrong, I'm letting you know it's going to cause problems. But I have your back."

The next day in the yard my homeboy tells me that I must take a punch in the face from a Mexican or they are going to stab me.

I looked at Robert to see what he had to say and yelled. "No, I'm not wrong. Fuck them Mexicans!"

The shot caller for the White's was a dope fiend. His name was Micky, straight Mexican sympathizer. Since the Mexicans had all the dope on the yard, Micky went along with all their decisions. Luckily, the whole incident blew over and was squashed in the end. A few weeks later Robert and I are getting some water. As we passed the weight pile, I noticed this Mexican, who couldn't of been more than 19 years old.

"Robert,"I whispered, "Look at that youngster. He's acting all hinky."

"Come on," Robert replied, "Let's go watch on the other side of the weight pile."

The whole yard is about the size of a football field. Surrounded by a paved track. There are pull-up bars, volleyball court, tables, and a weight pile that's surrounded by a chain link fence. Everything is spread throughout the yard.

As we're watching this kid slowly make his way over to the volleyball court, he takes a knife out of his pants and sneaks up behind this older Mexican. He stuck that knife through that older Mexican's neck. That youngster dropped that older Mexican and calmly walked off like nothing happened.

I look over at Robert and he said, "Let's get out of here, Dawg." We didn't make it twenty feet before the alarm started buzzing.

"Everybody down!" The tower yelled while he chambered his gun. Robert and I got face down on the ground in 115 degree weather for two hours until the medical staff walked out on the yard, placed the guy on a cart and took him out of the yard. Then everyone on the yard was strip searched ten at a time and escorted back to their cells. After we came off lockdown everything went back to normal. The victim had run up a dope debt he couldn't pay. Prison politics, if you're late paying a drug debt, be vigilant cause you're liable to get a knife stuck through your neck.

Every day was the same routine, work, exercise, and check in with the homeboys. Level 3 facilities are not too tough. I was certain I'd catch a third strike within my first year in prison.

A few weeks after we were let off lockdown, I got into another fight, but with a white boy this time. It started inside of the weight pile. This older guy took two of our dumbbells without asking and I felt disrespected to the point where I just punched him in the face. I was right below the gun tower.

"Get Down!" The tower yelled.

We both sprawled out face down as they placed us in handcuffs. This old timer says to me, "Hey youngster, what's up?"

I just ignored him. Later we talked on the yard and he apologized for taking our dumbbells without asking.

That incident raised my points to over 55, which made me a level 4.

The point system is designed to place inmates on specific yards. With level 4, being the highest, and 1 being the lowest.

"Mr. Curtis. You have a bad attitude and you're a program failure." My counselor explained to me. Seven months after arriving at Centinela State Prison, I was shipped to a level 4 prison, Corcoran State Prison.

I heard nothing good about Corcoran, since landing at Centinela. Corcoran has the notorious S.H.U. facility (which is pronounced shoe) and stands for Security Housing Unit. The types of inmates housed in the S.H.U. facilities are: Validated gang members, high profile P.C. and violent inmates.

For instance, if you're charged with battery on an inmate, you'll do 32 months in the S.H.U. Throughout most of the 1990s, the notorious S.H.U. was under investigation. Correctional Officers were staging fights between inmates. In some cases they shot and killed inmates for not stopping after they fired warning shots with the block gun. When I arrived at the S.H.U., my cellie Lefty ran down the rules to me.

"Chris, when you go to committee you have to convince the administration that you have a problem with the black inmates." Which wasn't hard to do.

The reason for this is so you'll land on the black's yard, with the northern Mexicans. Security Housing Units are segregated: Whites & Southern Mexicans on one yard, and Blacks & Northern Mexicans on another.

The yards in the S.H.U. are tiny. We call them hard yards. They are about the size of a standard garage, concrete floor, surrounded by block walls, with razor wire on top, then you have the gun tower. The C/Os know what time it is. "Curtis, are you ready for yard?" A C/O says to me. Knowing I can't say no. There is going to be a fight and they can't wait to see it.

I must go to the yard and wait for a black inmate to come out, and then take off on him. The crazy part is the block gun has to go off three times before I can stop fighting, or my cellie will try and kill me when I come back to the cell.

You can hear the block gun go off in the cells. After the block gun goes off three times, they chamber a round in the Mini-14. You stop fighting then or they'll shoot YOU.

The whole time you're fighting, several C/Os were watching you from the tower, betting on who'll win the fight.

Correctional Officers were eventually brought up on Federal charges, but the officers beat those charges in court. Even after one of their own testified against them.

Before I arrived at Corcoran State Prison, C/Os were a lot worse. New arrivals who came to Corcoran were literally beat down coming off the state bus by the C/Os. The Officer had taped over their ID Badges, so they couldn't be identified.

Not everyone was beat down of course, but several were.

When I landed in 1997 you could feel the tension as you were greeted by the staff in R&R. These C/Os could be dangerous. It's really all about respect though. You just have to pick and choose your battles with the C/Os.

Corcoran has 6 yards. Two S.H.U. yards, two Level 4 yards, one level 3 yard, and a level 1 yard. These level 4 yards are totally different than the yard I came from. Right when I stepped on Corcoran's level 4 B-yard, I mumbled to myself, "Now this is prison." You could literally feel the evil presence on the B-yard. Me and four other inmates coming from R&R didn't even make it to the orientation building before an alarm went off. Two Northern Mexicans were stabbing one of their own. The C/O in the yard gun tower fired two shots from his block gun, stopping the two Mexicans from hurting that inmate anymore. The yard had just been let off lockdown the day before.

I sat in orientation for a few weeks before finally being cleared for the yard. This being my first level 4, I didn't know what to expect. They moved me to 4 block the following night after a bunch of inmates were released from the hole, bringing with them a bunch of kites, along with a hit list.

Kites contain information for the yards shot callers, giving them orders, and other information on what to do, who to stab, etc. Most kites coming from the hole say who to stab or run off the yard.

It just so happened that my new cellie was on the list to be removed from the yard. So as soon as he came home from work, I just beat him up. I wasn't about to stab him with two strikes, in my own cell. I'd never get away with it. By the time the C/Os arrived blood was all over the cell. I had no chance to clean it up. They sent me to the S.H.U., for battery on an inmate. That's when I ended up with Lefty.

At my first hearing the captain said, "You're lucky that inmate didn't press charges against you."

I thought to myself, *What could I do? If I didn't do it, I would been on the list.*

Six months later I was released to the A-yard. I received another job in the kitchen and a month later I became a cook.

A couple months after I arrived there was an incident involving the White & the Black inmates. This whiteboy bought dope from a black inmate, which is not allowed. Whites are in no way to drink after, let alone buy dope from them, or any other business.

Well, this white inmate was late paying this black inmate for the dope he bought. The black inmate went into this white's cell while he was sleeping, and they fought. You can't fight another race without permission. And even if you ask for permission, you won't get it. Every race deals with their own. That's just prison politics. This being level 4 made a huge difference. Either there was going to be a riot, or the blacks were going to stab that inmate who went into the white's cell.

One day Lefty comes banging on the dining hall door, "Chris, find some weapon stock so we can make some knives."

"Don't trip," I replied, "I'll meet you on the track during chow."

"You can't walk out of the chow hall carrying weapon stock," Lefty cries, "You'll get busted homeboy."

"Dawg, don't jinx me. When you see the me come out of the dining hall with the CTQ cart, meet me by our building. "

Lefty gave me a concerned look and took off across the yard alking back to the building then added, "Be careful." CTQ Carts are used to carry meals to inmates Confined to Quarters (CTQ), which can be for a number of reasons. That inmate is either sick, drunk, etc.

So here I am in the kitchen with seven blacks, three Mexicans, and me. The cooks and scullery workers come in at 12 PM to prepare meals. The linebackers and line servers arrive right before the evening meal. Lefty had the day off.

I started searching the kitchen for loose metal that I could break off. It had to fit it down my pants, so I could smuggle it out of the kitchen. If I got caught, I'd be struck out and sentenced to life in prison.

The kitchen has four grills and four ovens, with two dining halls connected to the kitchen. There's a cop shop between both dining halls that has windows to see all around and inside the kitchen, and dining hall.

It didn't take long for me to find metal we could use to make some knives with. The light bulbs were covered with a metal protective cage. The thickness was the size of a pencil, which was perfect. Easy to sharpen, easy to bend, and strong enough to where it wouldn't break. The light covers were the size of a coffee can. The only problem was that they were directly over the grills where the blacks were cooking. I'd have to grab them before the table wipers and the linebackers arrived, or there would be too many C/Os in the area.

With time running out I said, "Excuse me." As I pulled a table up next to the grills. I hopped up onto the table and yanked two light covers off the light fixtures, jumped down, and headed for the bathroom in the back. I had to flatten them by jumping up and down on them.

Right away I noticed the blacks staring at me. G-rock, the shot caller for the blacks watched me through the bathroom window. "What ya doin?"

As I'm making a ton of noise jumping up and down on these little metal cages, I look up, "Nothin," I replied. "I just need these."

G-Rock walked off. I picked up my weapon stock, and stuck it down my pants.

As the line servers come in for their shift they all lean up against the grill watching the blacks talk amongst themselves. G-Rock walked up to me. "What's that metal for?" G-Rock asks.

As he asks I don't even look at him, then I turned and replied, "It's really none of your business!"

"That whole issue with one of my people running up in that whiteboys cell was squashed." G-Rock explained.

"What ya trippin' on then?" I replied

"Well, ya stealing metal out of the kitchen," G-rock replied.

"This is fucken' prison G-Rock." I was almost yelling now "I'm not here for selling bibles."

G-Rock laughed, "You one crazy wood." And he walked off. My only concern at this point was G-Rock could send some youngsters after me before I got the metal out of there. You just never know.

As they start to run the evening meal I go out into the dining hall to check the Kool-aid container. I see Lefty walking up to grab his tray.

"Here goes." I mumbled to myself.

Lefty looks at me and I give him the thumbs up. Lefty starts shaking his head. I ignored him and headed into the kitchen to grab the CTQ cart.

When I pushed  cart through the kitchen Lefty looked down to the ground shaking his head. As I walk by him I say, "Stop doing that homie. You're going to jinx me."

I know why Lefty was worried. Officers were always posted out front of the chow hall, doing random searches as inmates left the chow hall. He thought I 'd get busted.

As I get close to the door I start to get nervous. As I'm pushing the cart through the front door there is a sergeant in a conversation with a couple of C/Os. So I keep pushing the CTQ cart without even looking back, hoping they don't stop me. Right when I get about 20 feet down the track I hear a cop yell, "Curtis! Come back here. You know we're supposed to search before leaving with that cart."

"Oh no! Are you kiddn' me." I muttered to myself as I push the cart back for them to search it.

This C/O opens the cart looking behind all the trays and says, "Next time, stop so we can search you." And shuts the door. This officer didn't even search me. I took off and I'm halfway to 2 block when Lefty approached me. He has a big grin on his face, "You're lucky homeboy." As I hand him the weapon stock.

The following day the blacks were trippin' the yard was full of drama. Lefty and I were watching our shot caller and the black's shot caller. The whole time our shot caller is looking over at us. We were laughing so hard, we almost fell over.

As our shot caller walked over to us, I knew we would hear it, "Chris," He said, "Why did you let them see you grab that light cover?"

"I really had no choice. There is no way I'm getting caught in a riot without a knife."

He didn't even respond to my answer. He just walked off towards the building.

"Lefty," I asked, "Do you think he's mad at us?" We both just laughed.

The shot caller decided that someone would stab a black. If the blacks started a riot, we'd all be strapped with knives on the yard. The plan was all set for after third draw.

A few days before as third draw ended Lefty and I buried our knives on the yard. Lefty was paroling soon, so knives in our cell was a bad idea. Lefty and I moved in together a few days before all this went down.

A few days later we're playin' handball on the yard when we receive word that it was going down. I lit a smoke and walked with Lefty to the spot where we buried our knives.

"Chris," Lefty says all serious, "Look Dawg, If you fall

down get up as quick as you can, and don't let these Blacks surround you or me."

"Okay Homeboy, sure," I replied.

We're watching this white guy follow this black guy who has no idea he's about to be stabbed. I felt bad for about a second. The whiteboy ran up behind the black guy and stabbed him over and over until the gun tower started screaming,"Get down!" As you heard the block gun fire.

It was all over in about 15 seconds. Medical carted off the black guy, and took the whiteboy to the program office.

Lefty and I are looking at each other, waiting for all he blacks to get up and start rushing all the whites, but they didn't do anything.

Lefty paroled before we even came off lockdown. I was bummed to see him leave.

My new cellie came from a Level 3. His name was Johnny. Johnny was a red headed Irish boy from Fresno. We became close over the next few years. Johnny was always reading his bible in the cell. While I sat there watching my little black & white TV, smoking Buglar cigarettes, and that's all I ever did. I had about three years left on my six year term when Johnny arrived in my cell. I didn't have much contact with my family and I was barely holding on to any kind of hope. My life was out of control, even in prison.

Johnny got me a job working in the main kitchen, so we left for work at the same time. Right after breakfast we all lined up out front of work change and waited to be escorted to work. One morning Johnny woke me up with a startled look on his face, "Chris, get up! You're not gonna believe this but I'm going to tell you anyways. When I got done washing my face I looked over at you, and sitting against the wall next to you was a demon or something. Just staring at me."

I sat up in my bunk waiting for Johnny to start laughing. But he just stood there with a shocked look on his face. "Johnny, are you kiddn' me?" I replied.

"No, I'm not," Johnny whispered.

Johnny got up on his bunk while I got ready for breakfast. I washed my face, made some coffee, and lit a smoke. Then sat on the toilet waiting for them to run chow. It was the weirdest feeling hearing something was sitting next to you.

During the whole day I thought about what Johnny said. I mean, first if someone says a demon, I thought about why someone would believe something like that, you'd have to of had some kind of experience in your life.

When I was nine or ten years old, I saw something that gave me the chills to this day when I talk about it. My parents were still together at this time, and we were living on Morningside St. Behind our house was an old orange grove that stood between the 55 freeway and a track of homes.

Dad would take my brother and me snow skiing a couple times a year, in the Big Bear mountains. We always waxed our ski's the night before we left. This night dad told me, "Chris, go get your ski's so we can wax them."

I was gone, running through the living room that led to the hallway to our rooms. When I opened the hallway door and looked up there was an image of an old lady at the end of the hallway looking at me. I froze staring at this ghostly figure. The only way I could explain what it looked like, is it tingled in the air, with a green tint. I must have froze for only a second before turning back and running the same way I just came from.

Of course no one believed me, but I know what I witnessed that night. To this day I am not surprised about any story I hear about ghosts, etc.

As I thought about this unloading trucks on the back dock of Corcoran's main kitchen, I worried about what this all could mean.

A week later I started reading the Bible along with Johnny. And the more I read the more I started changing for the better. Along with me changing came my family too. My family could see that I was being sincere.

Looking back I see the difference it made. The six years passed by fast. One of my hopes was that Renee and I would get back together. I'd call Renee and ask if we could get back together when I was paroled but she didn't know. So I just kept hoping that I would have a chance to raise Brooke and Cory.

Johnny was paroled about a year before me. He had high hopes for his future like me. Johnny had kids too. He planned to raise them and stay out of prison. Like Lefty, I was glad to see Johnny leave. Johnny had a huge impact on my life.

My next cellie ended up being the shot caller. His name was Bo. He'd been doing time since the 80s. Bo was a little different from my other cellies. He turned 50 when I lived with him, but he was in good shape. Back in San Quentin in the 80s he was a boxer. When you looked at Bo you could see the danger in his eyes.

Bo was also from Orange County, and told me every day, "Chris, you have to do good out there. You get busted again, you'll be in here with me for the rest of your life."

Almost all the older homeboy's were doing life in prison under California's 3 Strike Law.

Not too long after Bo became my cellie I called home for Christmas. My mom's side of the family always met up at my Aunt Lynn and Uncle Mike's, in Villa Park. As I was talked to my mom my Uncle Ryan got on the phone, "Chris, how ya do in?"

"Good, How are you?" I replied. We talked for a few minutes, and Uncle Ryan says, "Has anyone come to visit you?"

"No, Uncle Ryan. It's kind've far." Uncle Ryan replied, "Send me and your Aunt Maggi a visiting form, and we'll come visit you."

I was stunned when he said that. I've been in prison for 5 years, and none of the family has come to visit. Not only that, Uncle Ryan barely even knew me. He married into the family in the early 90s. I went back to my cell and sat on my bunk in shock.

My outlook on life grew brighter every day. I had hopes for my future. Uncle Ryan, Aunt Maggi, and my mom came to visit me a month later. I was nervous at first, but after the first ten minutes I was laughing and having a great time. They couldn't believe how healthy I looked, but I felt even better. Aunt Maggi and I played cards while we all talked. I was surprised to find out that Aunt Maggi and I weren't even related by blood, shocked me. Aunt Maggi was always there for me, mom, and my brother.

When I told Uncle Ryan I had a black & white TV, he insisted on buying me a colored TV. Uncle Ryan gave me his phone number and told me to call him in a few days. Life was good. Maybe as good as it has been for as long as I could remember. I had no desire to use drugs. I also constantly read the Bible. I couldn't wait to get out of prison and live a normal life. Most importantly, I wanted to be a good dad.

Uncle Ryan helped me call my daughter Brooke, and Cory, using a 3-way. Renee was now living in Phoenix, Arizona. I still had no answer concerning our relationship. With only three months left of my sentence, I figured there was no hope.

We were all trying to figure out where I would live when I paroled. Mom's place was too small. Uncle Ryan wanted me to come live with him in the San Bernadino mountains, but the parole department wanted me right back in Anaheim where I committed my crimes. In the end, we decided I would go live with my brother in Anaheim Hills.

On September 11, 2001, we were locked down due to a stabbing in the chow hall. It was the biggest knife I'd ever seen in prison. It looked about a foot long with a handle made from a sheet. Every time that Mexican was stabbed it gave me the chills. When the cops yelled for everyone to get down, I grabbed my tray and ate my food while they cleared the chow hall.

As a critical worker during lockdowns, if your race is not involved in the incident, you still go to work. Especially if you work in the kitchen.

As I was waiting to go to work in my cell, I had my TV on watching the news. I had a cigarette and a cup of coffee in my hand, watching one of the Twin Towers on fire. I didn't have my headphones plugged in so I couldn't hear what they were saying. All of a sudden I see something crash into the side of the building, sending debris falling towards the ground.

I couldn't believe it. At first I thought I must be watching a movie, until I seen Matt Lauer on the Today Show, explaining what was happening. I yelled out the door, "BO! Come check this out."

Bo was out on the tier passing out breakfast trays to each cell. He's a morning tier tender, better known as a porter.

"What's up?" Bo replied from the first tier. "Turn on the TV." I explained, "And turn it to NBC."By that time everyone was yelling out their doors about what was happening on the news. Two planes had been highjacked and flown into the twin towers. The officers and the inmates in the dayroom are now watching the news. Everyone was shocked about what they had seen over and over, as NBC kept playing the tape of terrorists flying commercial planes into the side of the World Trade Center.

New York had just been attacked by some crazy ass terrorist over religion, and in a few months, I was due to parole.

The night before I was paroled, I couldn't sleep. I thought I would be rearrested at the gate for some other crime I had committed in the past. For the last six months, there wasn't a day that it didn't cross my mind. On the morning of January 1, 2002, I was paroled. As usual we were on lockdown. They popped my cell door. "Curtis, you ready?"

I tossed my cigarette in the toilet, grabbed my belongings and was out the door. Aunt Maggi and Uncle Ryan would pick me up at the front gate.

Me and three other inmates sat in R&R as happy as could be. I thought to myself, "I made it and will never commit another crime again or use drugs."

# CHAPTER 12

Driving home with my Aunt and Uncle was nice. We stopped at Denny's restaurant. As soon as we walked through the door I had a relaxing feeling. After eating in a hostile environment for so many years, this was a definite change. I couldn't wait to eat my favorite breakfast: over-easy eggs, hashbrowns, and sausage. That was one delicious meal.

As we're all sitting at the table Uncle Ryan nudged me in the arm, "Christopher, isn't this nice?"

"Uncle Ryan, it sure is."

After everything my Aunt and Uncle did for me I had nothing but love and respect for them. They really did care about me. I was grateful to have them in my life.

As we're eating I hear cell phones ringing all around the restaurant. It was a trip for me. When I went to prison in the mid 90s cell phones were expensive. We'd always buy chipped cell phones.

Chipped cell phones were hooked up illegally, and most criminals in the 90s could buy them for $50. You'd have to have special cables and a computer program. Motorola Flip phones were popular. To break into the phone all you'd have to do was press #08, and you could change the phone number and password. Now owning a cell phone was like owning a pager. Everyone had one.

Soon as the food arrived I ate like an animal. Not even realizing how I must've looked. You learn how to eat fast in prison. For one, they rush you out of the chow hall (sometimes only giving you 5 minutes to eat), and other times some random act of violence will happen. I've seen plenty of inmates stabbed or sliced while eating or leaving the chow hall.

It was peaceful eating in a restaurant and refreshing. After all those years had passed, I felt loved. I feeling I hadn't felt in many years.

We drove towards my brother's pad in Anaheim Hills. I'd be there until I could afford my own place. My loving mother had planned a little welcome home party for me. Uncle Mike, Aunt Lynn, and my Grandparents. I hadn't been in contact with any of these family members in at least ten years. You could tell by their demeanor that they didn't wanna be there. The whole welcome home made me uncomfortable. I'm almost positive they only came because Uncle Ryan made them. I never really knew my andparents. I couldn't tell you much about them except that my grampa was a World War II veteran.

My nephew and niece were great. They were excited to have me in their home. You could see it in their eyes. I became attached to them fast.

Before I was paroled my mom asked me what I wanted for dinner, I said, "Pizza, Pizza, and more Pizza." I LOVE pizza. Mushroom and pineapple is my favorite pizza. I literally could eat pizza every day of my life.

Everyone sat around for an hour and then left. Mom was so happy to have me home. Also I was finally able to meet her new boyfriend. She had been dating him for a year or two. Right away I knew he was a good guy. His name was John, and he took good care of her, unlike that idiot Bill.

Uncle Ryan and Aunt Maggi were the last ones to leave.

"Christopher," Uncle Ryan said, "If you need anything let

me know."

I could see how concerned they both were when they left, but I would prove to everyone that I could be a good person.

I was given the hay closet for my clothes, and the living room couch for my bed. It was nice to be around my brother again. I'm not sure hat his wife, Catherine, thought about me, but I would find out soon enough.

My niece Lisa, and nephew JR, loved the fact that I was living there. Oh, there were also two dogs and a cat. Arbuckle, the black lab was totally cool. I couldn't get enough of him.

The very next day I had to meet my parole officer. This is mandatory upon your release from prison. You have twenty-four hours to check in or they'll violate your parole and send you right back to prison for one year.

My first parole officer was a really nice woman. She asked me a few questions, drug tested me, then advised me that I would be receiving a new parole officer at my next visit. Since I was on high control parole, they were adamant about me being a gang member from a skinhead gang. I insisted that they had it wrong. Yet, the Anaheim Police Department said differently. Besides that, I didn't care. I wasn't going to give them any reason to violate me, so they could think whatever they wanted.

After visiting the Anaheim Parole Department, my next stop was the D.M.V. My sister-in-law was nice enough to take me there too. For the first time in my life I received my driver's license - only took me thirty years. My mom was meeting me at the house later on, to take me to Marty's. I think Marty's just might be part of our family.

I decided to call Renee. I really wanted us to be a family. Me, Renee, Brooke, and Cory. I received the most shocking news. Renee told me that she had another kid named Ricky. Ricky was not even a year old yet. I couldn't believe it. I still didn't care though. Brooke and Cory needed me around them. Plus, it's my own fault for going to prison in the first place.

Before I hung up the phone I asked Renee, for the tenth time, "Are we going to get back together, or what?"

Renee replied, "Chris, I don't know."

I finally realized I was wasting my time and that I would have to be the best father I could from a distance. After our conversation I talked with Cory and Brooke. I explained to them that I was out of prison now. They both wanted to know when I was coming over. With them living in Phoenix, Arizona, it would be a while. I couldn't wait to see them though.

My mom showed up just before the sun went down. I jumped in her car and we drove to Marty's. I was glad to get out of that house. I'd never had a drink in Marty's, so, I was excited to finally be able to experience it. I've always thought about how it would feel to go inside and have a drink, and play darts with my mom.

As we drove towards Marty's, I thought to myself, *Did I forget my Bible in my cell?* Realizing that I hadn't read it since leaving prison.

Mom made a right into Marty's parking lot, suddenly changing my thought to excitement. I was seconds away from sitting at the bar with my mom for the first time in my life.

When I walked into the bar I noticed several people who I grew up with, Jene, and a few others. Jene lived a couple of houses down from my dad's house on Sacramento St. I had a great time sitting at the bar with Jene and my mom. With two Coors beers in my stomach I felt better than ever. Jene was always close with my brother. She still looked good. Her brother Pat died from an overdose a couple years before I paroled. Which you could almost blame on my dad's house. Pat was at our house every day when we lived on Sacramento St., getting high. Every time I looked at her I felt a little guilty.

Being around Jene after all these years brought back good and bad memories. Just two weeks before I was sitting in a cell in Corcoran State Prison. I felt fortunate to be enjoying a free life without being under the gun, day after day.

Next thing I know I see this pretty girl come through the front door. I couldn't stop looking at her. As she started playing darts with some friends, I asked, "Mom, who's that girl playing darts?"

"Which one, Chris?"

"The one with the dark hair."

"Oh, That's Gina. Come on I'll introduce you to her."

I was nervous as we walked across the bar. I've been locked down for six years in prison. I felt my palms get moist. Next thing I know Gina and I had been playing darts for hours, laughing, and having a great time.

Gina had grown up in the city of Orange, and her parents, like mine, spent a lot of time at Marty's. Gina was almost 40 years old, nine years older than me. She was attractive, and her smile melted my heart.

Hours later as we're sitting at the bar my mom approached, "Come on Chris. I have to get you home."

Before I could say a word Gina replied, "Kathy, I'll take him home."

We stayed at Marty's until well after midnight, playing darts and talking. Gina knew all about my situation before the night ended. She knew I just paroled, what I went to prison for, and what my plans were moving forward in life. On the way to my brother's she gave me her phone number.

As she drove away I lit a smoke and leaned against my brother's truck. I couldn't believe it. What were the chances of me meeting this girl. I couldn't help but smile. All of a sudden I saw this black dog running down the street towards me. "Arbuckle, what're you doing outside?"

Arbuckle looked at me, turned his head like he was trying to figure out what I just said, and followed me up the driveway.

The next morning I had a positive outlook on my future. I'd be a success, beating the odds. The rate for inmates returning to prison is around 85%. Most inmates get violated within the first month, sentenced in a Kangaroo court, for minor violations. I refused to be a statistic. I'll never see the inside of a prison cell again. As I rolled a smoke, I realized how empty my stomach was. So I went into the kitchen to find some breakfast. I opened the pantry door, grabbed a box of cereal, milk out of the refrigerator, and sat at the dining room table.

As I started to eat Arbuckle strolled up, sitting right next to me, giving me those puppy dog eyes. I've always loved dogs, and being around Arbuckle was nice. When Catherine left the room, I set the bowl down on the ground and let Arbuckle have the rest of the milk. I couldn't let him down. He wiped the bowl clean with his tongue. Arbuckle was one happy pup.

When he finished I picked the bowl and washed it in the sink, then set the bowl inside the dishwasher. Soon as I finished I heard Catherine behind me, "Good morning Chris."

"Morning Catherine, how ya doing?"

"I'm good Chris. I've gotta run some errands. What're your plans?"

I thought for a second, then replied, "Going to go buy a gun with my gate money."

Catherine looked at me with a horrified look on her face.

"Hey, I'm just kidding, Jeez!"

"That's not funny," Catherine replied.

"Well it kinda is," I mumbled. "Actually I'll work out and then look for a job."

"That sounds better," Catherine muttered as she walked out the door.

I had the house all to myself. I lit a smoke and walked into the backyard with Arbuckle right behind me. He took off across the yard, grabbed an old teddy bear in his mouth, and brought it back to me, dropping it at my feet. It was obvious I had to play with him. I threw the teddy bear across the yard a dozen times.

After that got boring I took Arbuckle in the garage with me and worked out. Talk about a cluttered garage. This place reminded me of a straight tweeker pad.

My brother had started to build a room for me, which was far from completed. My favorite part of the garage was the weight bench. Soon as I started doing burpees Arbuckle thought it was playtime. He jumped all over me, trying to lick me and all that crazy stuff dogs do. After Arbuckle finished being crazy I continued to work out.

After burpees I did bench presses. It felt great to lift

weights. They took our weights while I was in Corcoran State Prison. The prison system decided inmates were getting too healthy and removed all the metal weights. That didn't stop us. We just used water bags for weights, which worked out well. You just had to be careful not to injure yourself.

After exercising, I showered. It felt odd not looking through bars. I've heard stories about the way people feel after being in prison for long periods of time. You never really understand it until you're released.

After I decided to call Michele. I'd missed her over the years. As usual, I got an answering machine. So I called my old buddy Carl, from grade school. We talked awhile and decided to go to the batting cages.

As I waited out front Arbuckle was running around acting stupid. Smelling and pissing on everything. I just laughed at him. Carl drove up and parked in the driveway. I was trippin' on him. He looked exactly the same except for his short hair. Carl always had long black hair growing up. "How ya do in, Chris?" Cory asked.

"Good Carl, good. You haven't changed a bit, except for your hair."

"Yeah, just a little older and wiser."

"Let's get out of here and have some fun." I replied. I chased Arbuckle back into the house, and we headed for the batting cages.

As we're driving Carl says, "You've been gone a long time. What're your plans?"

"You know what Carl I'm going to get a job and live a normal life, for once."

Carl took a long drag off his smoke and replied, "I might be able to get you some work."

"That would be great. I'll never touch drugs again. I'm done with that shit, Carl."

Carl pulled into the parking lot and parked in front of the batting cages.

"Chris, I think we did enough drugs on Sacramento St. when you lived with your dad to last us a lifetime."

"Yeah, I hear that. I didn't stop there just kept going until I shoot two people and went to prison." I lit a smoke and looked out the window. "That household corrupted all of us Carl. Will killed himself, Pat overdosed, and you, me and Jed were wasted youth. You know I sat in prison day after day thinking about how dad started me and Jed on cocaine."

We both stepped out of the car and walked to the counter. The cashier took our IDs, and handed us bats and helmets. We hit balls for an hour or so. It was nice to hang out with an old buddy.

Carl dropped me off, explaining that he would call me in a few days.

When I walked into the house my nephew JR ran up to me, "Uncle Chris! What ya doin?"

"Not much, little buddy. What's up?" Then I grabbed him and threw him over my shoulder, spinning him around until he begged me to stop. By then, Arbuckle had joined in on the fun, barking, and jumping up and down.

"Do you wanna go play some basketball out front?" JR was out the door before I finished the sentence. By the time I made it out front JR was already dribbling the ball down the driveway. I ran up behind him and stole the basketball, and slam dunked it. "Now what, sucker!"

My brother had bought the kids a little basketball hoop, that was adjustable. You could raise it, or lower it. His house was at the end of a cull-da-sac, and JR had dragged the basketball hoop out into the street. JR had a ton of energy just like me when I was his age. As we're playing several kids came over and joined in. It was me against all the kids. We had an awesome time.

When I finished playing I decided to call Gina. I started thinking maybe she wouldn't want anything to do with me. She's never been to jail or anything like that. She didn't answer the phone, so I left a message. I hoped she would call me back.

Surprisingly, Gina returned my call. We laughed as we talked about all the fun we had. Then decided to meet at Marty's the following Friday. Every day until Friday dragged like an upcoming parole date. I had a great time with Gina and ouldn't wait to see her again.

Friday morning finally arrived and I was excited. I couldn't wait to play darts at Marty's. I couldn't remember having as much fun, as I did the week before. I worked out extra hard, did laundry, burned daylight, and waited for the evening to come. Halfway through the day I received a call from Michele. She gave me directions to her apartment in Anaheim, and I explained to her that I would find a ride over there in a few days. I couldn't wait to see Michele. She and Gerrid had a baby girl while I was in prison.

As I hung up the phone all my homeboy's warnings filled my thoughts, "Stay away from all your old friends, youngster." I just always looked at them and replied, "Don't trip homeboys, I won't."

I've always been hard headed, and was certain I would never get into any more trouble, let alone use drugs. Uncle Ryan had a lot of confidence in me, and I couldn't let him or my mom down. Plus I had Brooke and Cory to think about. Committing a crime would make me a third striker (25-to-life in prison) was out of the question. Not me, never. I was out in the yard smoking a cigarette when mom pulled up in her car. I tossed my cig in the gutter, and jumped in. "Hi, mom!" I said as I kissed her on the cheek. We talked about what I'd been doing. I explained to her that I hung out with JR, played with Arbuckle, and worked out. Being thrown back into society was actually a shock.

When we walked into Marty's, Gina hadn't arrived yet. I was glad because that gave me time to drink a few beers. I hadn't talked to women in years and was a little intimidated by Gina. She was smart and had her life together. I felt out of my element.

I sat with my mom and drank my favorite beer, Coors. My mom was great. I never realized how cool she actually was to hang with. I could see now why my parents came to Marty's for all these years. My dad had stopped coming to Marty's after he went to jail in the late 1980s, for selling cocaine.

In no time at all I was playing darts, and listening to music. I recalled how several weeks prior I was locked down in prison over an inmate being stabbed over a drug debt. Now I was playing darts, waiting on my future girlfriend, and couldn't be any happier.

All sorts of people filled the bar after the sun went down. Jene, and some other kids. Everyone was drinking and laughing, having a good time.

After awhile, I went out front to smoke a cigarette and get some fresh air. As I'm watching cars drive by on Tustin Ave., I spot Gina pulling into Marty's parking lot. Soon as she spotted me, she smiled, and I smiled right back. I walked up to her so I could open her door and said, "Hi, Gina."

"Hey you. How ya doin'?" Gina replied.

"Better since you showed up."

Gina started to laugh, and replied, "Stop it! I could really use a beer. How bout you?"

"Well, Gina. You're at the right place." She started laughing again.

We both walked into the bar together, ordered a couple of beers, then sat and talked about everything. I even explained to her the whole shooting incident. The funniest thing about explaining to someone how you shot two people is their response. Most people ask, "Did you kill them?" Or some response like that. Gina just listened and said, "Well, you paid your debt to society, and under the circumstances, you had no choice. People don't run the streets selling bibles. They're selling drugs, stealing cars, robbing stores, and sometimes killing people. And you never really know what a person is capable of doing, until it happens."

Gina changed the subject. She wanted to go bowling. Her friend from work, Debra, was taking her son to Regal Lanes bowling alley. I was all for it. I spent the better part of my childhood hanging around Regal Lanes.

Regal Lanes is about a five minute walk from Marty's. Behind Regal Lanes is the entrance to the storm drains, where my friends and I used to explore. This bowling alley also had video games and pinball machines. I couldn't wait to pick a bowling ball after Gina mentioned it.

Debra and her son were already there when we arrived. Gina and I rented shoes and found a couple of bowling balls. As we paid for a lane, I recalled all the memories I had in this place. Her son was around 8 years old. I talked with him a little. Kids are such a trip. We bowled for a few hours, then left.

We headed straight back to Marty's and sat at the bar, and drank for the rest of the night. By the time we left it was already early Saturday morning. We helped the bartender close up for the night. We'd known the family who owned the bar for years and it was late so we helped out. When we hopped into Gina's car she muttered, "I don't think I can drive all the way to your house let alone mine."

"Well I can't drive. If I get caught drunk driving, I'll spend the rest of my life in prison."

"I know, that's why we're going to my parent's," Gina replied.

"Gina, we're really going to your parent's? Won't they trip on me?"

Gina looked and replied, "They live right down the street, and I have my own key."

"Okay, let's go." I muttered.

On the way to Gina's parent's I was already worried about having to meet them in the morning. I had no clue what to expect or what I would say to them. Five minutes later, as we pulled into her parent's driveway, all the lights in the house were off. I was glad they weren't awake.

Quietly we stepped through the front door. Right away I noticed several cats at our feet, purring. This one cat looked like a poddle. It was gigantic. I was trippin' on this cat. I picked him up and said, "Look at this hinky looking cat. He's coming with us."

Gina laughed, and replied, "You're weird."

As we went down the hallway to the back bedroom, the hardwood floor was creaking with every step. Gina flipped on the light as we entered the room. The room was nice, with two nightstands, fresh paint, and a queen size bed. The room even had its own shower.

The next thing I know it was morning. All I remember is trying to put the moves on Gina and her punching me. Six years in prison, what'd she expect. I looked around the room and Gina was gone. "Son of a bitch!" I whispered as I spotted that big-ass cat looking at me. He looked even bigger in the morning.

There was no way I could leave. I went into the bathroom to wash my face. I didn't know if it was okay to smoke, so I lit a smoke and was blowing it out the bathroom window. Next thing I know Gina opens the door, "What're you doin' Chris?"

"I'm smoking a cigarette."

Gina gave me a weird look and replied, "Why are you smoking in the bathroom?"

"Didn't know if it was cool to smoke in the house, so I'm in here so I an blow it out the window."

"Yeah, you're kind've weird and it's okay if you smoke in the house."

"Where are your parents at?" I asked.

"They're waiting for you so we can eat breakfast."

"Son of a bitch! Are you serious, Gina?"

"Quit being a whimp and let's go eat." Gina replied.

At first I felt awkward sitting there with her parents, but after Gina introduced me, they seemed nice. Gina's mom made me feel comfortable. Her dad just gave me that look the dads give to their daughter's boyfriends. But besides that, her parents were alright. They didn't drill me with a bunch of questions. We just all talked while we ate.

After we finished eating I thanked her parents, and we left. I couldn't get over the feeling that I had just been paroled from prison. All this was Like a dream.

Later on that day Michele called to tell me, her, Ann, and a couple of the homeboys were meeting at the Sports Bar, off Orange Thorpe, in Anaheim Hills. Located like five minutes from brother's house. So I told Michele that I would meet them there.

When I walked through the front door of the Sports bar I thought, "Now this is a bar." People were dancing, playing pool and standing in groups all over the place.

The bar was like three times the size of Marty's. It might have even been a nightclub. I spotted Michele and everyone else seated at a table near a pool table.

Matt, Michele, and Ann were all laughing at something when I walked up. I practically grew up with Michele. Ann is one of Renee's best friends and was at the hospital when Brooke was born. Matt and Chuck both hung out at Dina's before she went to prison. It was strange seeing all these people after six years.

An hour later every one of us was drunk. I was dancing with random girls for the first time in my life. I look over as I am dancing and notice Matt and Chuck arguing with a bunch of guys by our table. I stopped dancing and strolled over to see what the problem was. As I got closer I heard Matt cussing and BAM! He socked one guy right in the face. Kicking off a mini riot, right there in the Sports Bar. We've all spent time in prison, so it wasn't nothing new to us.

Our only problem was we're outsiders, and we didn't have the numbers so it was just the three of us against who knows how many. I remember hitting a few people before being socked in the eye and then Michele pulling me out the door.

Ann, was stabbed in the hand and bleeding all over. As we ran towards the car I heard sirens in the distance, obviously heading to the scene of the incident.

"Chris," Michele yelled "Come on. You have two strikes. We've gotta get you outta here!"

I had Michele drop me off at my brother's friend's house. Ann went to the hospital, and everyone else went their separate ways.

That knife cut Ann's hand deep. I had a swollen eye, and everyone else seemed alright. Soon as I sobered up I started trippin'. My shirt was all bloody, my eye was swollen, and I had to see my parole officer in the morning.

The following morning I sat in the parole office with a

black eye waiting to be called. I kept mumbling to myself, "I'm going back to prison." Thinking the Sports Bar had cameras and just being released from prison, they would identify me easily.

When my name was called I walked through the door leading to my parole officer's office. I can't remember this parole officer's name, but she turned out to be really cool.

"What happened to your eye?" She asked.

Having all day to think about it I came up with the best possible excuse. "Well, my brother has this big dog named Arbuckle, and I can't seem to get him to stay away from me until I throw him his little bear to fetch. Arbuckle came running back with his toy in his mouth, dropping it in front of me. I leaned over to pick it up as Arbuckle jumped up in the air, slamming his big-ass head into my eye."

My parole officer looked at me with curious eyes, and replied, "You know what, Mr. Curtis. That's a good one." And she continued on with our visit. I just sat there as she told me about their expectations, and advised me again, that I should be receiving a new parole officer because of being on high parole. I wasn't too happy about losing her. Later you'll understand why.

# CHAPTER 13

Within 60 days of parole from prison, I had two jobs, a car (that Gina helped me buy), and an apartment Gina and I had rented in the city of Orange, located right off the 22 freeway. My new life was awesome.

My brother helped me land an excellent job with Miller Pipeline. It paid $18 an hour, plus benefits. Me being the new guy meant I didn't get a full 40 hours a week. So when I wasn't working my Union job, I was working with my cousins Jeremy and Jake, my Aunt Maggi's sons.

Working with my cousins was a big help. They both looked out for my best interest. There are drugs everywhere, especially on construction sites.

One day I went to grab a tool from Jake's tool bin and this guy Willy, who worked for my cousin was doing meth inside. Out of nowhere Jeremy appeared looking at Willy, then at me.

"Willy, are you giving Christopher drugs?"

"No, Jeremy. He just walked up right before you." Willy cried.

Jeremy looked at me, then back at Willy and added, "If I

ever find out you're giving him drugs, you'll never work for the Workmans again."

Jeremy gave me a concerned look, then walked off.

I knew everyone did drugs. They're all over the place. Prison itself is full of drugs. But I kept reminding my cousins that I was done using drugs and not to worry.

A few days later I received a call from Renee, "Chris , I'll be at Michele's in a few days."

I hadn't seen Cory or Brooke since before prison. This meant I would have to get permission from my parole officer. With me being on high control parole now, it would be highly unlikely.

When I got the call from Renee, telling me she had arrived at Michele's, I told my cousins I had to leave. I was going to see my kids for the first time in 6 years. Michele lived in West Anaheim.

The apartment complex was run down in a gang infested area, but a cheap place to live. Soon as I entered the complex I noticed Brooke, Cory, and Emily, playing in the courtyard with some kids. I stopped to watch them play for a couple seconds.

I noticed Brooke started to argue with some kid and then squared off, like she was ready to fight, so I ran over. Cory noticed me first and ran up to me. I gave him a hug. Brooke just stood there looking at me. She never knew me before I went to prison. Cory ran off to tell Renee I was outside. I knelt down to talk to Brooke, "Hey beautiful! How are you?"

With a really shy voice, she replied, "Okay."

I couldn't help but smile. Michele always said she was shy. It felt good to finally be able to see them all. I grabbed Brooke's hand and we walked inside.

When Renee saw me walk inside with Brooke, she stood up and gave me a hug. She was still as beautiful as ever. We talked about what I was doing with myself since paroling. Right away she started hinting about us getting back together, which made me angry.

I asked her a dozen times if we were going to get back together, and she always replied, "I don't know." Which I figured meant that she didn't want to, or that she didn't have the heart to tell me no. So I moved on and met Gina.

My intention going to Michele's was to take Cory and Brooke to go get something to eat. But I did something to Cory that I regret to this day.

I became so angry by seeing Renee with her new baby and then her talking about us getting back together that I grabbed Brooke and left. Cory loved me like a father. I wrote to him every week, just like I did Brooke. I took Brooke to lunch at McDonald's, then to the park. We had a great time. Brooke just sat in the passenger's seat so well behaved. It felt amazing to finally spend some time with her.

When I brought Brooke home, Renee was irritated with me. I could see it all over her face. She had every right to be mad at me. Before I left I said to Renee, "I asked you several times if you wanted to try and work out our relationship, and you always said no."

Renee just walked off.

On my way home from work one day I received a call from Kristle. Soon as I heard her voice I knew it was her. I missed Kristle the most out of all my homegirls. We were really close until I went to prison. Kristle went on to explain to me how she was doing.

She went to school and became a nurse and was now employed at a hospital in South Orange County. She also told me Chucky was in a drug program called Delancy Street. Located in San Francisco. They were separated but still kept in contact.

Slowly I started talking to my old friends again. Some were sober, some weren't. But I was certain I would never use drugs again. So why couldn't I hang out with them? Plus, if I ever got busted again for anything, I'd be sent back to prison for the rest of my life. Not to mention, I would be letting down my family, and I couldn't do that.

Gina came home from work one day telling me about her friend Debra. I guess Gina discovered her friend was doing meth at work. And when she didn't have it, she got depressed.

So I mentioned, "Gina, I could score meth anytime."

Gina replied, "No way Chris."

Yet, I insisted it would not be a problem, "Gina, I'll be fine, don't trip!"

That was the biggest mistake of my life. How could I ever of thought that it would be okay? I grew up selling and using drugs. Not even a month later I was selling meth for extra money. I wanted to buy a motorcycle, and with a car payment, child support, and rent, I would never be able to afford it. I figured I would sell drugs. Why not? I didn't use drugs anymore. I'd make a bundle of cash in the process.

Soon as my friends found out I was selling meth, they were concerned. Michele and Mick, whom I had known since I started running the streets, were on me all the time. Gina, she had never been around it before so she didn't realize what could happen. Also, I said it would only be for a short time.

I worked all day and then sold drugs at night. Of course my cousins knew nothing about it. In the beginning, I stayed low-key. I kept nothing in my apartment and was really cautious.

About a month later I was drunk and decided to smoke some meth. I'm not even sure why. When I arrived home the next morning and told Gina, she was not happy about it. One night as I walked through Mick's hotel room door he shouted, "He's Baaaack!" His girlfriend Sue added, "Chris! You're high, huh?"

"No" I replied, "I'm not."

"Chris, how long have we known you?"

"Well," I mumbled, "I guess the cat's out of the bag." It steadily got worse from that point on.

One Saturday I was working on my Aunt Maggi's house with my cousin Jeremy. The house was in an upper middle class neighborhood in Mission Viejo, in South Orange County. Jeremy had his whole work crew there helping out. We were installing drainage pipes, so the backyard wouldn't flood during rain storms.

This guy who lived across the street pulled up into his driveway with a GSXR-750 motorcycle in the back of his truck. The bike was in bad shape, yet with a little time and money, I could fix it up. So I made my way across the street to have a talk with him.

"You wanna sell that bike?" I already knew he used meth, which I had plenty of.

"Yeah, I'll sell it Chris."

"Okay, but you can't tell my cousins I bought this with Meth!"

He said for me not to worry.

I only paid a half-ounce of meth for the bike. Soon as I got home that night I called Mick, "Mick, do you know anyone who works on motorcycles?"

Mick told me that he knew this guy, Derrik. I got his phone number and called him.

A few weeks later Derrik came over to pick up his last payment for repairing my motorcycle. He looked bummed out when I was talking to him, "Are you alright Derrik?"

Derrik kind of stumbled answering the question. Almost like he was embarrassed. Then looked down to the ground and started to explain, "I was doing all this work on other motorcycles for this guy. When I completed my end of the bargain, he kicked me out on the street. Without even paying me."

I thought for a second and replied, "What kind of work were you doing?"

Derrik told me about this chop shop the guy was running, located in some industrial park by the Anaheim Stadium. Derrik also explained that there were over 20 motorcycles all fixed up, with good plates and pink slips.

Derrik was about 22 at the most. He actually reminded me of myself when I started running the streets. This person who ran the chop shop was clearly taking advantage of him. So I started thinking to myself, then looked at him, "Derrik, what you say if I could get your money from him for you?"

Derrik got all excited, "You could get all my money from him?"

I reached into my pocket and said, "Well, let's smoke a

little meth, and we'll talk about it."

I got Derrik nice and high and asked everything I could about the chop shop. Who hung out there, were there guns in the shop, and what time did it close. I needed all the information to get a good understanding of how the place ran.

After he explained all he knew about the shop, I replied, "Derrik, I'm goin' to rob the place. There must be thousands of dollars worth of motorcycles in the place. He won't call the cops because they're stolen bikes. I'll even give you a quarter of the cash."

Derrik, looked at me like he had seen a ghost, then said, "Well, I don't wanna go!"

"Derrik, I don't want you to go. When this is all over, I'll give you your money and you can leave the area."

"Where will I go Chris?"

"I don't know Derrik, but get the hell away from this place. One more thing, Do not talk about this to anyone!"

"I won't Chris." Derrik muttered.

When I arrived home Gina was already sleeping. I got into bed and stared at the ceiling, thinking of a plan to rob the chop shop. If I could pull this off, I could come up with at least $20K. I could payoff the car Gina helped me buy and buy a brand new motorcycle.

When I woke up the next morning I had nothing but the chop shop on my mind. The first thing I did was call Mick, "Hey, you wanna make some quick money?"

"Sure," replied Mick.

"Okay, I'll stop by your room after work."

That night at Mick's, I explained the whole situation to him, "Mick, this lame who runs this chop shop used Derrik, then kicked him out on the street."

Mick looked up from playing his video game and replied, "Why doesn't Derrik, deal with it himself?"

"Mick, for one it wasn't his idea, it was mine. And two, he's scared. Plus, I need the money."

Finally after talking Mick into helping me, I said, "I need a gun."

"Oh god," Mick cried, "This idea is getting worse and worse."

"Mick, what're we gonna do, rob him with our cellphones?"

"Everything is always a joke with you Chris. Plus, I don't like the idea of you having a gun."

I responded, "Mick, I'll get it one way or another."

"I know, Chris. But you have two strikes now, and any crime you commit will give you a life sentence. Every week that goes by you seem like your old self. You were doing good. Why get involved with all this crap again?"

"Look, after I do this, I'll stop."

"Yeah, I heard that before Chris."

Finally I replied, "Well, I have to get home. Gina is waiting on me." I walked out the door.

As I strolled down the hall of the hotel, I thought to myself, *soon as I pull this off, I'll stop selling meth.*

When I walked through the door to my apartment, I was tired. Not only from work but my conversation with Mick. Gina was watching TV and gave me a look that said she was mad.

"What's wrong with you Gina?"

Gina picked up the TV remote and turned the TV off. I knew I would have to listen to her for the next twenty minutes.

"Chris, You're acting different lately."

"What do you mean by that?"

"I'm not sure Chris, you're just different."

Quickly I changed the subject, "What's for dinner?"

"Whatever you want Chris." Gina replied, as she went into the bathroom.

"Pizza sounds good to me."

Gina yelled from the bathroom, "You live on pizza." I mumbled to myself , "I thought I lived on meth but whatever."

I ordered a mushroom and pineapple pizza then took a shower.

As I was showering I started thinking, *Maybe everyone was right. I'd let so many people down if I got busted, and went back to prison.* I just kept telling myself that it couldn't happen to me.

That night I couldn't sleep. While Gina was in dreamland, I stared at the ceiling. Maybe I should've went into a program after I got released. Next thing I know my alarm was beeping. Time to go to work. I had to be at the shop at five in the morning. We were working in Palm Springs.

Slowly I sat up and lit a smoke. Then went into the kitchen to add another scoop of coffee to the coffee pot. Gina always made the coffee too weak, and this morning I needed a strong cup of coffee. It seemed like we drove more than we worked at Miller Pipeline. I guess that's the benefit of working a Union job. I couldn't stand sitting around. I'd rather be on the move.

I walked into the bathroom, threw my half smoke into the toilet, brushed my teeth, washed my face, and grabbed a cup of coffee. Then I put the leftover pizza into a zip-lock bag, grabbed a couple of sodas, stuffed it all into my lunch box, and was out the door.

While I was on my lunch break I received another call from Kristle, "Chris, my Uncle Jay is paroling in a few days."

"That's cool Kristle." I replied as I stuffed pizza into my mouth.

"Oh, and my friend Kim is having a party. She lives in Huntington Beach. It's a sober party. You're still sober, right Chris?"

I almost choked on my lunch before replying, "yeah, of course I am."

"Well, you better be or I'll kick your ass."

"Okay, calm down." I smiled. "Kristle, I'll be there unless something comes up." And I hung up the phone.

I ate the last piece of pizza, downed a soda, lit a smoke and stepped out into the hot Palm Springs sun. It felt like I just walked onto Centinela's prison yard in the middle of summer. A couple of days later I asked Derrik to take me to this chop shop. I needed a good look at this place.

"Derrik, don't make this guy suspicious. I'm going to act like I want to buy a motorcycle."

"Alright, Chris," Derrik muttered.

When we got to the shop in my Honda Civic, Larry, the guy who ran the shop was out front with his pit bull. This dog was huge. I'd probably have to shoot this dog right from the start.

Larry looked at me weirdly. I held out my hand to shake his and said, "Derrik is telling me that you have good deals on some bikes."

Larry grabbed his big-ass dog by the collar and led him into the shop, "What kind of money are you looking to spend?"

"I don't know. Maybe 3 or 4 thousand dollars." I explained. The whole time I'm talking to him I'm checking out his shop. The shop had about ten new motorcycles parked in a row and several toolboxes lined up against the wall.

The shop was clean, with an office in the back. I lit a smoke and said, "Larry, thank you for your time. Can I stop by later?"

"Sure," Larry replied without even looking at me.

As Derrik and I walked to my car, I added, "This guy is a jerk. He has all those bikes, and he can't pay you?"

"Nope," Derrik replied.

"Well Derrik, don't worry. He'll get what he has coming to him."

I started my car and we drove off. While we were driving I called Mick to see if he was ready. Mick told me to meet him at a car wash in East Anaheim. So I dropped Derrik off at his friend's house.

When I drove up to the car wash Rick was all tweeked out with junk scattered all around his car. This car wash was a do-it-yourself deal, right in the middle of a gang infested area. You pay like a buck fifty to spray and wash your car and another dollar to vacuum it out.

I parked my Honda Civic in the stall next to his and walked over. As we're talking I look over and spot a bald headed white boy drive by, staring at us.

"Mick, are you expecting anyone?"

"No," Mick replied.

"Do you have that gun on you?"

Mick looked at me as he dug around in the front seat of his car and asked, "What're you trippin on, Chris?"

"Some guy just drove by staring at us. Do you have a knife, or anything we could use as a weapon?"

"Chris, you're trippin!" Mick yelled.

"Well, I'm going to get my screwdriver."

By the time I got back from my car, Tiny (who is a skinhead) had Mick on the ground beating the hell out of him.

I ran up to them and yelled, "Get the fuck off my homeboy before I stab you."

Tiny looked up at this big-ass screwdriver in my hand and said, "Chris, you're wrong. You're going to be in trouble for this."

I just stared at him as he jumped in his car and left. Mick was in trouble for something that happened at Chino State Prison. Mick wasn't even on parole anymore. Actually I didn't care anyways. I've known Mick for many years and wasn't going to let him get beat up, ecially while I was standing right there. I knew I would be hearing about this, but I didn't care.

Mick and I threw all of his belongings into his car and sped off to his hotel room. When we arrived I lit a smoke and sat on the couch, "What's up Mick? Why are they after you?"

Mick ignored me and walked into the other room. I already knew why they were trying to find him. I just didn't say anything. When Mick was in Chino Prison on a violation, he was in Palm Hall (which is Chino's hole) and they wanted him to stab his cellie when he was about to parole. Mick told the shot-caller no. I would've told him no too. That put him on the hit list, better known as being in the hat.

A few days later Renee called me, "Chris, I'm at Michele's with the kids."

I explained to her that I would come over later.

"Chris, Evil is here." Renee replied. "He's Tiny's homeboy."

"Son of a bitch! Is Michele and him together?"

Renee whispered, "I don't know Chris. What're you gonna do?"

I pulled my car over and lit a cigarette, to think about the whole situation, and replied, "I'm coming over to see the kids, and whatever happens, happens."

I hung up the phone and got back on the road. Mick and I had to meet to work out the details. For sure we needed a U-haul, and this whole chop shop scenario had to be dealt with soon. So I headed straight to Mick's hotel room. When I knocked on the door no one answered. Right away I knew Mick had a change of heart. I jumped back into my car and headed to my motel room. I had rented a room at the Tampico, off State College Blvd, in Anaheim.

I wasn't there but a couple of minutes when Mick called, "Chris I'm sorry but I can't make it. But do you remember Mark?"

"What do you mean you can't make it, Mick! Are you fucken' kidding me?"

At this point I just wanted to get this whole thing over with.

"Tell Mark to meet me at the Tampico. I'll be out front. Alright, Mick?"

When I hung up the phone I was furious with Mick. After everything that happened at the car wash. Getting myself involved in his mess. Now I have to go through a bunch of drama just to see my daughter. I should've let Tiny beat the crap out of him.

A half hour later Mark drove into the Tampico's parking lot. I watched him slowly drive through the parking lot trying to spot my room. It wasn't like I didn't know Mark. I just didn't think he was capable of what was about to go down. Out of all the people we knew, Mick sent this lame.

I opened my motel door and got Mark's attention, and waved him up to my room. I took a drag off my smoke, looked around the parking lot, then flicked my smoke over the balcony. It landed on an old beat up Ford Pinto.

"Hurry up!" I yelled from on top of the stairs.

As Mark slowly made his way up to my room. I sat Mark down in one of the only two little chairs in the room and explained the whole situation. I thought back to my younger days and said, "Mark do you remember when Matt shot Flaco in the foot in one of the downstairs rooms?"

Mark looked at me like I startled him, so I added, "Forget I even mentioned that Mark. Did you bring the gun Mick gave you?"

Mark stood up and lifted up his shirt, pulling out a Glock -9, handing it to me.

I grabbed it, pointed it toward the floor, popped the clip out to find it fully loaded. I tossed the clip on the bed, pulled the slide several times to make sure the chamber wasn't loaded. Then picked up the clip and popped it back into place. "I got my gun. Where's yours?"

Mark sat back down on the bed and replied, "Chris, I don't need a gun."

"Are you fucken' kidding me, Mark! What're you gonna do? Look at him? There's a pit-bull in there will eat your fat-ass!"

I was getting upset, but what could I do? Mark was a lame. It's not his fault.

Finally I told Mark to follow me. Most importantly I asked him to stay behind me. I've got two strikes and a loaded gun.

Five minutes after we're on the road I look behind me and Mark is gone. Right away I pulled into an alley and tossed my gun into a bush. I was calling Mark all sorts of names as I jumped back into my car, and headed to the 7-Eleven off of La Palma and Sunkist. I didn't know what to do at this point.

I walked up to the pay phone at the 7-Eleven and lit a smoke. As I sat there smoking it hit. I picked up the phone and dialed Michele's number.

"Michele? This is Chris. Is Evil there?"

"Chris... ," Michele replied, "Just let all the drama die down, then come over and see Brooke."

"Just put him on the phone."

I heard Michele mumble a few words, then Evil muttered, "Hello."

"This is Chris. Look, lets go out into the alley behind Michele's apartment, and we fight one-on-one to squash that incident that happened with me and Tiny at the car wash. Cause I need your help to rob this chop shop."

Evil didn't even hesitate one second, "We don't have to do all that. Just come over and we'll work it out."

"Yeah?" I replied.

"Serious, just come over, Chris."

I drove back to the alley to retrieve my gun and headed towards the 91 freeway to get to Rachell's.

As I am speeding down the 91 freeway towards Michele's with a gun in my waistband, I muttered, "Here I go again... driving around with a gun on me. Son of a bitch!"

As I exited the 91 freeway onto Euclid St. I made a left. I knew Evil wouldn't get scared. They won't let you be a skinhead, being weak. As I made a right into Michele's neighborhood, I couldn't shake the feeling that I was being set up. I knew for a fact that Evil would have several homeboys hanging around. I'd have to be vigilant. I had my Glock-9, and I'm sure they had theirs too.

I parked my car a little way down Michele's street so I could get to her apartment through the alley. As I strolled down the alley I kept thinking about all the homeboys telling me in prison not to hang out with my old friends.

When I came to the stairs leading to Michele's courtyard, I placed my hand on my gun under my shirt. The stairs were only twenty steps. When I arrived at the top I looked everywhere only to spot several black kids running around. Then I made a left towards the pad. They wouldn't try anything hinky inside of the apartment. Michele wouldn't let that go down.

Brooke answered the door after I knocked. With her shy little voice she said, "Hi." I gave her a big smile and hug.

Evil walked up behind Brooke, "When you're done talking to your daughter, I'll be in Michele's room." I just nodded and followed Brooke to the couch, and we sat down.

Me, Brooke, and Cory sat around talking for a while. I still felt terrible for leaving Cory that day. I was confused about what I should do and after awhile I headed to Michele's room.

Michele's room was littered with all sorts of papers, clothes, and a computer on the desk. Michele, Evil, Joker, Pirate, Casper, and Renee were all smoking meth.

Joker and Casper I didn't know. Joker as well as Pirate, were skinheads. Pirate and I have known each other for several years, and this was my first time meeting Evil. I explained to them what Mick did, and Evil replied, "You should've let Tiny finish what he was doing." I didn't reply to that comment. Mick and I were still friends, and nothing could ever change that. Plus, I don't get involved in prison politics, especially on the streets. My goal is money, and that's it.

Within an hour we were all smoking meth. When I got high on meth I turn into a comedian. I had everyone laughing so hard they were practically rolling on the ground. It was a trip. Almost like we'd known each other forever. A few hours ago these guys wanted to kill me, and now we're all buddies.

Evil and I went into the bathroom to talk. I didn't want Renee hearing about this robbery. She'd just use it against me in the coming days.

I explained the whole situation to Evil. He was all for it. We both decided to bring Joker along. It was all set for the following evening after I returned home from work. We'd steal a U-Haul and head for the shop.

After Evil and I had our conversation, I headed back into the living room. The kids were laid out on the floor asleep. I turned off the TV and sat on the couch. I was high as a kite on meth. I just sat there recalling everything. That night I didn't even go home. We all sat around smoken' meth, laughing. Gina called every ten minutes and I just ignored her calls. It was like I didn't care anymore. How could've I gone from, I'll never use drugs again, to being high and planning a robbery? In my mind I kept telling myself that there was nothing wrong with me. meth had taken over my life again, and I couldn't see it.

Early the following morning I raced home. I had to be at work in Chino with my cousin's. They were building a warehouse across the street from Chino State Prison. I dropped off my gun, grabbed my work clothes, and headed to Chino.

When I arrived at the work site Jake, Jeremy, and Willie were all huddled up in a deep conversation. I stepped out of my car and lit a smoke, "What's up, guys?" I asked as I walked up to them.

"Someone robbed the tool shed," Jake replied. There were two shipping containers that my cousins used to lock up all their tools. Right away I looked at Willy and I ain't stupid. They both know that game. Willy got his buddy to scope out the place out and prints would be all over the place. The locks were cut with a blow torch by his Mexican buddy down the street. He had the job, and his buddy robbed it. His fingerprints were there since he worked there. I wanted to shoot Willy and his friend and bury them in that lot.

After everyone got to work I mentioned to Jeremy, "You know Willy and his buddy robbed you guys, right?"

Jeremy didn't wanna hear it. Willy is their meth connection on the job site. I'm assumed Jeremy didn't wanna stir up any trouble. Yet, I would wait and when the opportunity arose, I'd get Willy and his buddy. And no one would ever know.

Willy had paroled from prison a couple months before me. He was a big guy who sold meth. He roamed around the job site like he was all that. I couldn't stand him.

After work I drove to Michele's as quick as I could. was already late thanks to traffic. I parked in the alley, grabbed a change of clothes from my trunk, and headed inside.

Michele had all the kids on her couch, scolding them for running around the apartment, yelling at the top of their lungs. When I came through the door Michele saw me, and said, "Brooke's dad is here. You're all in trouble now."

I looked at Michele and replied, "Why do you have to make me the bad guy, Michele? All you kids go outside and play!"

All the kids ran out the door without another word. I jumped into Michele's shower, cleaned up, then went into Michele's room. Everyone was there from the previous night. Once again, they were all smoking meth. I grabbed the pipe, filled it with meth, to keep it going for another twenty minutes. Me, Evil, and Joker went over everything concerning the chop shop. There could be no mistakes. You could never predict the outcome of a situation like this one. Most importantly, you don't want to get shot.

We headed towards the shop. We'd steal a U-haul truck near the shop, located by the Anaheim stadium. We found a U-haul right away, a block from the shop. Evil explained to Joker to steal the truck, then meet us at the shop. Without another word he was out the car door.

"Evil," I added, "Look, there's a pit bull inside. If we have to shoot it, we'd better get out of there fast."

Evil lit a smoke then handed it to me, and lit one for himself, "Chris, the way I see it is if we have to shoot anyone, we got ten minutes to beat feet."

Evil had a 45 automatic, and I had a Glock-9. Both guns would make a lot of noise that wouldn't sound like fireworks.

It was already dark when we pulled into the parking lot. There were three shops on one side of the parking lot and three on the other. They faced each other.

When I parked I realized that the parking lot was empty, which seemed odd. We both looked at each other and said, "This is looking better and better. No one here, fewer problems."

Evil put his smoke out in the ashtray and chambered a round into his 45 handgun.

"Hold on Evil," I said, "I'm going to knock on that back door and see if that dog barks."

I stepped out of my car and walked up to the door, then knocked a few times. I waited a couple minutes, and then waved Evil over. Next to the door Evil clipped the lock with bolt cutters. As the garage door rolled up, Joker drove into the parking area and lifted the metal door. Evil looked inside, and said, "The place - not often you find it empty, homeboy!" whipered Evil.

"Son of a bitch!" If Mick would've came like he was supposed to, everything might've worked out fine.

Within a month after this failed robbery attempt, I was selling a half pound of meth a day. Me and Woody, who I met through Mick, were working together. He lived in Santa Ana, the next city over from Orange.

I also became wanted on a PAL warrant. Which stands for Parolee at Large I gave my parole officer a dirty test for meth. I even left Gina, and my mom was calling twenty times a day. So I just bought a new cell phone. The streets had sucked me in again.

For the next several months I ran the streets. Picking up right where I left off before going to prison.

# CHAPTER 14

Over the next month I met so many people. First I met a guy named Dakota. Like Evil and I, we became instant friends. I could trust Dakota, unlike most tweekers who roam the streets. Dakota had a wife named Tiffany. They'd both been to prison but were now off parole. Tiffany was nothing less than a sweetheart to Dakota. Like me she had two strikes and had been fighting her sobriety for years. Their apartment was in the city of Orange. I met Dakota from a friend of Michele's, Helen. Helen is about 5 ½ feet tall with blonde hair, and good looking.

One night Helen and I were driving around the city. I was trying to score some meth, and as usual, Mick was being a flake. So Helen introduced me to Dakota.

I started looking for homeboys with the same interest, money. I didn't wanna be like I was in the 90s before going to prison when anything I wanted I just took it or robbed people because I thought I had something to prove. Now I was on a whole new trip: pay back anyone who did me wrong in the past, and be honest and upfront with everyone. Unless I knew their intentions were to do me harm or my homeboys.

After that incident at the car wash, I couldn't stay mad at Mick. To this day I would still do the same for him. One night Mick had his buddy Woody over at his hotel room. I was smoking a cigarette, listening to Woody complain to Mick about this guy who owed him a thousand dollars. As I'm listening to Woody describe this guy who has a blue 914 Porsche, I butt into the conversation.

"So, by chance if I run into this guy and get your cash, what do I get?"

Woody handed Mick some dope, then looked up at me, "I'll give half, Chris."

"Mick is it alright if I get Woody's phone number?"

Mick replied as he blew a big cloud of smoke, "It's up to Woody." Mick mumbled.

Woody gave me his cell number and left. I kid you not, a few nights later I'm with this guy named Kirby, who I met through Helen as well. Kirby is explaining to me about this guy named Mark, who wants to buy some meth. Mark lives over the hill from Eisenhower Park in the city of Orange. Kirby and I drive over there.

As I am in the house with Kirby, who I barely know, I see this guy drive up in a blue 914 Porsche. I have no gun and think, *Son of a bitch. What am I gonna do?*

I'm looking at these three guys who are all buddies, wondering how I will pull this off. Mark's living room has two couches and is kept up real nice. There is nothing I could see to use as a weapon. Finally I said, "Mark, can I borrow a screwdriver?"

"Sure, Chris, go look out in the garage," Mark replies. I stood up and walked out the front door. The door leading into the garage was directly to the left of the house's front door.

I searched for the biggest screwdriver I could find and called Woody. Of course I got his answering machine, so I left a message. I walk back into the pad, screwdriver in hand, "You know my buddy Woody?" This guy sees the serious look on my face, and the screw driver in my hand, and just looked to the ground.

I knew right then the answer to my question. "Do you have Woody's thousand dollars?"

"Uh... No." He replied.

"Well, I'm aking your car or stabbing you with this screwdriver. What's it gonna be?"

The whole time I'm hoping these guys don't jump me. Surely the three of them could beat me up if they had the heart.

After the owner of the Porsche looked to his two friends for any sign of help, he realized he's on his own.

He sputters, "Alright, take the car."

My heart was pounding. I explained to him that when he paid Woody. I would return his car to him and gave him my phone number. Then I told Kirby I would pick him p later.

The following morning I received a call from Kirby, "Chris, I'm nothing like that guy you took the car from. That guy is always having problems with people over money."

As he explained this to me, I'm shaving in my hotel room. "Kirby did he call the cops?"

"No," Kirby replied. "He said he knows who you are and that he don't want no problems. He also said he would get the money to you or sign over the Porsche to you." I thought, *What do you mean he knows who I am?*

"When you left he said that's Chris Curtis. He must've just got out of prison. He went to prison several years ago for shooting someone. Did you just get out of prison?"

I dried off my face and looked into the mirror thinking, what the hell am I doing? Then replied, "Kirby, look, I'll come by and we'll talk later." Then hung up the phone.

I didn't wanna have this conversation with Kirby. But, a week later I rented a room from Kirby. He turned out to be another loyal friend. His house was directly across the street from the Thrift Store, by the Orange Circle, in the city of Orange. As much as I hated the city of Orange, this house was perfect, with three bedrooms downstairs, and one master bedroom upstairs, which was haunted, so it stayed empty. Besides that, it was a great place to live.

A couple of days after I took the dude's Porsche, I received a call from Woody, "Chris, that guy who owes me money called me. He said he's going to sign over the Porsche to me. Did you really take his car?"

"Yeah," I replied, "I ran into him the other day. I tried calling you, but you didn't answer. So I threatened him and his friends with a screwdriver 'cause he didn't have your cash. Then I ended up taking his car instead. I told him he could have his car back when he came up with your money."

Woody started laughing, and from that day forward, we were friends.

It's difficult to find homeboy's on the streets with your same motives. You have productive homeboys like Woody and I, and you have several who are too tweeked out on meth to function correctly. I can't say much because I was like that in the 90s. Within a month Woody and I were selling a pound of meth every other day. And as the weeks passed we sold more and more. Woody had paroled from prison around the same time as me. One day he says to me, "Every time I ask somebody about you, they either say they love you or they're scared to death of you."

"Woody shut the hell up."

"Chris I'm serious."

I paused for a second as I snorted a big line of meth, gagging on the taste and replied, "Woody I suggest asking someone from the early 90s the same question and see what they say."

"Yeah," Woody muttered, "Well this is 2002. Oh, I have this fully automatic AK -47 in front of me. Do you want me to buy it for you?"

"Hell yeah. Of course, I want that gun." I replied.

Now I had a TECH-9, Glock-45, and an AK-47. Not to mention all the other guns I had. I even bought a bullet proof vest. I stored most of these weapons in my storage unit off Glassell, in the city of Orange. Storage units are a safe place to store stolen property, guns, and drugs. I was collecting all sorts of rollaway toolboxes, stereos and things of that nature.

While I was at Dakota's one night this guy Benny dropped

by the apartment. Right away I recognized him from back in the 90s. Benny and his brother burned me for $500. I was waiting for him to notice me, but he didn't.

Benny was begging Dakota to sell him some meth. Promising him that he would pay him later. I'm just sitting there listening to his bullshit. As Dakota explained to him several times that he had no meth. I know Dakota is lying because I just handed him a big bag of meth. It was obvious that Dakota didn't wanna deal with this dude. Knowing he wouldn't pay him.

Benny gives up heading for the front door I jump up, "Benny, hold on for a second. I'll give you some meth. Are you positive you can pay me in a couple days?"

"Yeah, no problem. I just live right next door. Dakota will show you where I live."

"Come back in an hour Benny, and I'll hook you up with an 8-ball."

Soon as Benny left Dakota started explaining to me that he won't pay me back. I sat back on Dakota's couch and replied, "I did that on purpose homeboy. Benny and his brother burned me for some money. And when he doesn't pay me back, I'll take everything he owns."

"Chris, he lives right next door." Dakota cried.

"Dakota, don't worry. I promise he will never touch you."

Dakota gave me a concerned look and walked out to his little patio. At this point Dakota didn't really know me yet. I'd never let anyone harm my homeboy. Especially because of my actions.

While waiting for Benny to return, Dakota and I were taking apart computer hard drives. Hard drives have powerful magnets inside that you can epoxy to guns, bags, and whatever else you want to hide under your car. Those magnets are so powerful they could hold a brick under your car.

I bought a little 22-caliber handgun, and to be safe I glued a magnet to it so I could hide it under my car, along with a little black bag that I filled with dope. The theory behind this is if the public has access to under your car, you cannot be charged with a crime because the police cannot prove it's yours.

As I am letting the epoxy dry I heard Dakota yell, "Chris, your phone is ringing." I walked into the pad and hit the button, "Hello."

"Chris, it's me Evil. The cops raided Michele's pad, and I'm in the county jail."

I grabbed a smoke and lit it, then replied, "Are you serious?"

Evil was quiet for a second.

"Evil, how much is your bail?"

Quietly he mumbled, "A hundred thousand dollars."

"What the hell! Why so much?"

"Well I threw a 45 caliber gun out Michele's bedroom window."

"Where's Michele at?"

"She was arrested too." Evil replied, "But I'm sure she'll be out in a couple hours. Chris, can you bail me out of jail?"

"How will I ever come up with that kind of money." I muttered. "Look Evil, I'll try to figure something out. Do you know of a bail bondsmen we can work with?"

"Yeah, Evil explained. "I'm sure someone does in here."

"Okay Evil. Call me later."

As I hung up the hone I handed Dakota a bag of meth, "Dakota this is for Benny. I have to go." Then walked out the door.

I drove to my hot room at the Embassy Suites. A hundred-thousand dollars is a lot of money. I'd have to come up with ten thousand in cash and some collateral. Either way, I liked Evil and couldn't let him sit in there. He was there when I needed him.

I decided to call Woody to explain the whole situation to him. When I told Woody he replied, "You're really going to bail that dude out?"

"Yeah, Dawg. I'd do the same for you."

"Chris, we're both on parole. We'd never get granted bail." Woody explained.

I put out my smoke and added, "Woody, let's hope it never

comes to that. I'll talk to you later."

Most nights I stayed by myself. Sure I had the house in Orange. But that was used more as a storage unit and a place to meet up with people. Also I enjoyed being alone to think. Sometimes I would lay in bed and think to myself, *What am I doing?* But would justify my actions somehow. Every once in a while, I would be able to smell the county jail, lying in my hotel bed. It's a very distinct smell you never forget.

So many people were coming and going from the house in Orange that I didn t even like being there much. My cousin Jeremy was buying meth from me now, along with a couple of his buddies. I don't even remember how Jeremy found out I was selling meth. But I told him several times it wasn't his fault. Some of Evil's buddies came to the house as well. I'm suspicious of hanging around places with people who I don't know well. If the wrong person finds out where I live it could be a major problem. Next thing you know you're being robbed, or put into a position where you have to shoot someone.

A good example. I started selling dope to Tiny. He'd hand me a couple thousand dollars and say, "Call me when you score Chris and I'll come pick it up."

Well I'd be at my hotel most of the time by myself when he came to pick up his dope. I would have my Glock 45 in my hand behind my back when I answered the door. I'd say to him, "Lift up your shirt, turn around." To make sure he wasn't armed. "Your dope is on the table. No disrespect, but I have way too much money in here."

Tiny would laugh as he walked out the door. Tiny is way too big and scandalous to trust. He's at least 200, that's not even his healthy weight. I'd have to shoot him because he would smash me in a fight.

After Tiny left, I wouldn't stay long at that hotel. Matter of fact, twenty-four hours is the longest I'd stay at any hotel because any longer and you're asking to get busted, or worse.

Michele wanted to drive with me to the bail bondsman to work out the details of Evil's bail. In the end I ended up signing over ownership of my Honda Civic and agreed to make payments on the rest, which I'd never do.

Evil was let out at midnight. Me, Michele, and Renee picked him up at the 7-Eleven, down the street from the Orange County jail. Evil was one happy individual. We drove over to this pad that Evil knew about. This apartment was bust. I noticed it right from the start. I wouldn't be caught dead in this tweeker pad in the early morning hours. I don't know what it is about cops, but they're always raiding pads in the early morning hours. It never fails. Between 5 & 8 AM, Dina's pad was stormed by several cops.

Evil jumped to his feet still smelling like the county jail. I explained to Michele that it wouldn't be good to go with us. She got the hint and decided not to go.

On the way over I explained to Evil what was going on. How this Benny guy burned me for $500 years before, and that I fronted him some dope, knowing he wouldn't pay me back.

Evil asked, "Are you gonna beat his ass?"

I took a long drag off my smoke and flicked it out the window. "Hopefully it won't come to that Evil. For one thing I don't know who'll be there. But I know one thing for sure, I'm packing this rent a car with all sorts of his belongings."

When we arrived at Benny's pad, he wasn't even home. Although his garage was full of all sort of tweeker's, and some old gang-banger and his old lady. I could care less because I was going to pay this lame back for burning me.

Littered all over Benny's pad were all sorts of computers, toolboxes, and some other miscellaneous crap which I had plenty of room for in my storage unit.

"Chris," Evil whispered, "Are we gonna do this or what?"

I got close to Evil and replied, "I want Benny to be here. You know what, screw it!"

I stood up and pulled out my Glock 45, "Look, I'm taking everything I can fit in my car. Benny owes me money, and I'm not waiting for his lame-ass. Everyone stand up and lift up your shirts."

I had my gun pointed at the gangbanger. Wasn't too worried about the tweeker's. "Anyone of you have a problem with this?"

One guy replied, "No man. We're cool."

"Also, don't try anything stupid. I smoke a grip of meth, and I'll shoot you."

Evil looked at me giving me a weird smile as he was loading up the car.

As we were leaving I told them, "One more thing. If anything happens to Dakota, I'll come back and it won't end well."

I thought it would be safe if we unloaded all this stuff at my pad in Orange. The house was only five minutes away from Dakota's.

As we're approaching Kirby's pad I noticed car lights in my rearview mirror. So I passed the house to see if this guy was following us.

Sure enough it was the same black TransAm that I saw parked in Benny's driveway. Soon as I got to a stop sign, I let the car catch up to me. Then jumped out of the car with my gun in my hand, walking towards the driver side window. That gang-banger saw me coming and all I heard was tires screeching, as he punched the gas in reverse. So I took a shot at his radiator to scare him a little.

Evil was laughing. I decided not to go to Kirby's and we went to Kristle instead.

The toolboxes, and computers we took weren't $500 dollars, yet the experience was worth it.

The next day I drove to my storage unit to drop off all Benny's stuff. I couldn't even go home until I got a new rent-a-car. The cops might have a description of this car, plus that gangbanger and his homeboys could come looking for me too. That's one great thing about rent-a-cars. Every week you switch cars and it confuses the cops.

While I was tweeking around my storage unit I got a call from Chucky, "What's up Chris! How ya doing?" I was so shocked I stopped to light a smoke, "How'd you get this number?"

"Who else," Chucky replied. "Kristle gave it to me. I'm

living in Pocatello, Idaho. Come out here and visit. I know you're doing good right now."

Shocked again, I asked, "How do you know that?"

"Well," Chucky added, "You bailed Evil out. OH, and Jay paroled. He's at Kristle's."

Soon as Chucky said that I got another call coming in "Chucky, hold on. My other line is ringing. Matter of fact, call me later dawg."

"Hello."

"Chris, it's me Jay. How ya doing hinkerton?"

"How long have you been out?" I asked.

"Since yesterday. Come get me."

"I'll be there later. Is Kristle with you?"

"Yes Sir." Jay replied.

"I think she might be mad at me. I was supposed to go to some party in Huntington Beach. She knows I'm using meth again."

"So what! Come get me. I wanna use meth too homeboy."

As I shut the door to my storage unit, I replied, "Alright ay. I'll try and be there in a couple hours." And hung up. I jumped in my car heading towards Lance's shop. He was a buddy I met through Mick. His shop was down the street from Richland High School. I had to meet my cousin's friend there, Derry.

As I drove into the alley lined with shops, I noticed a guy at the end of the alley. Lance's shop was the second shop of eight lined up. With a parking lot on the left, and shops on the right. There's one way in and out. This guy just stared as I parked my car. When I stepped out of my car a dumpster blocked the view so I could grab my dope from under the car.

Lance's shop was hooked up with a security camera out front and a monitor inside his office. Which meant I could see who was coming and going. Lance lived in his shop, that was littered with all sorts of junk. You name it, Lance probably had it lying around. Lance had taught me how to do all sorts of illegal things on a computer, like making California Identifications and things of that nature, which really came in handy.

A few minutes after arriving I see Derry drive up in his truck. I watch him get out of his truck on the monitor and walk up to the shop. I've known Derry since I was a kid. He grew up with my cousins in Mission Viejo.

While we're all in Lance's office I'm weighing out an ounce of meth. I notice on the monitor, out of the corner of my eye, a whiteboy checking out my car. I'm clearly watching this guy on the security camera, "Derry," I said, "check this out! There's a guy looking under my car."

I throw all my dope in my bag, zip it up. Derry, and I take off towards the exit.

When I opened the door to the shop that whiteboy is reaching under my car, where I stash my dope, "Hey stupid! What're you doing under my car?"

The guy jumped up shocked. He was about my size, just a little younger.

"Oh," He explained, "I'm just looking for something."

With my cousin's best friend inside, and this jerk twenty feet away from me, I try to figure out what to do. As I'm thinking this Mexican guy starts to approach me from the end of the alley. As he's walking towards me I notice him slipping on black gloves, like he's going to beat me up or rob me.

I look at the whiteboy, and this other guy coming towards me, and reach under my shirt and pull out my Glock-45, "What, stupid!" I yelled, stopping him dead in his tracks.

That Mexican turned white a ghost and replied, "Hey, I'm sorry."

As I have these two guys at gunpoint, I hear the shop door open behind me, then Derry, "Chris, No!" As he's pulling me back from these two. Now Derry is standing in between us. "You guys better get out of here." They both took off back the way they came.

"These idiots were trying to burn me, Derry!"

Derry knew I just paroled from prison and I'm sure I just scared the hell out him. I grabbed my black bag and we split.

After that incident I decided that I would start hanging out in Lake Havasu, Arizona. Renee and my daughter lived out there and I was worried about being in Orange County. It seemed like I was constantly asking for trouble. I'd already got a PAL warrant, and it only takes one ignorant tweeker and I'd have to shoot someone. My life would change forever, and unlike the 90s, I wasn't looking for trouble.

I went around to all my homeboys who sold meth for me to let them know I would be out of town. I explained that I would come back once a week to pick up my money, and score more dope. That would give everyone plenty of time to sell theirs.

As I'm driving to my cousin's house in Mission Viejo, I received a call from the Orange County Sheriffs. Dakota had been pulled over in my rent-a-car. A major mistake on my part. I rented that in a desperate attempt to deal with an issue. I had all sorts of illegal items in the trunk of that car. A fully loaded TECH-9, stolen laptops, and a variety of other stolen goods.

The call came from an investigator inside the sheriff's department. "Mr. Curtis. We pulled a car over that in your name off Oso Parkway, in Mission Viejo. Inside we found a fully loaded TECH-9, with several other items. Would you like to come pick up your car?"

As I'm pulling into the driveway at Jeremy's house I replied, "I have no idea what you're talking about. And nooo...I will not be coming to get that car. Matter of fact, you can return it to the rental company for me." And I ended that call.

Dakota was going to jail, and there was nothing I could do. This made it that much easier to leave Orange County. Plus, Lake Havasu was a beautiful place to live. I could visit Brooke and Cory whenever I wanted. I still thought about what I did to Cory. It wasn't his fault Renee and I couldn't work things out in our relationship.

When I talked to Michele and Evil about going to Havasu, we decided it would be a good idea, especially after Evil got arrested again after only a few weeks of being out, which cost another $1000. I was shocked they didn't do a no bail warrant on him. After this I wouldn't be able to bail him out again. So Evil saw this as a good opportunity to get out of Orange County too.

After we packed up a rent-a-car, rented in Tiffany's name, we headed for Havasu. I already felt a release of pressure. There is nothing better than leaving Anaheim. I've done this move years before when I was supposed to start a new life, but instead, brought my screwed up mentality with me. Once again I was running away from my problems. The circumstances were a little different, yet still the same.

The drive to Havasu was great. We stopped at Desert Center, before taking Rice Road to Parker. Luckily it was dark as we made our way through the desert. Evil decided to dye his hair blue, which made him look crazy.

Renee heard us drive up and greeted us with a smile, happy to have us there. The house had two bedrooms and was a nice typical Arizona house with the normal gravel and cactus filled front yard.

The next day we got super high and relaxed. I unloaded my guns and put them away. No one knew where we were in Lake Havasu. It felt good to just sit back without having to worry about getting busted or even robbed.

Evil took off to Emily's with Michele. Emily is Cody's ex-girlfriend. Not only that, I shot two of her friends. Talk about a small world.

Later in the day I rented a room at Motel 6. Then found out that Emily actually worked there. She showed up at my room on her lunch break. I couldn't tell you how it happened, but we hooked up. Next thing you know I'm living at her apartment.

Chucky called me every day, asking me to come out to Idaho. I finally promised that I would make the trip. We hadn't seen each other since 1994. While I made plans to drive to Idaho, I first had to drive back to Orange County. I was running low on meth. I left Evil and Michele in Havasu, jumped in my car and headed back to Anaheim.

I fronted this guy Mitch a bunch of meth before leaving, so he could sell it while I was gone. Evil agreed to keep an eye on him in Havasu. With everything planned I had nothing to worry about as I headed home.

When I walked through the door Kirby was asleep. I was

back in the city of Orange. "What're you doin' sleeping?" I asked as I kicked the side of his bed.

Kirby jumped up startled, "Waiting on you." He replied. "I've been out of dope for two days."

I opened my black bag and handed him a bag of meth. "Fill the pipe," I said. "Did you collect all the money?"

"Yeah, all of it except John's and Sueann."

I met both Sueann and John through Dakota. Sueann is some tweeker girl who is a little scandalous but alright for the most part. John drove around Orange County in a 24-hour plumbers van and sold meth. He made me a lot of money, and was loyal. I almost had to beat him up a few times, but he learned fast.

"Has Woody come by?" I asked as I walked into the kitchen.

Kirby yelled from his room, "Yeah, he came by yesterday and I told him you'd be here today."

I look at the stairs leading to the master bedroom and reply, "Kirby, I don't see how you live in this pad by yourself."

I grabbed all the money and headed to see Woody. Ever since Dakota got busted, I knew those cops would be looking for me. I couldn't stay around for long in this county. Plus, Havasu was so much nicer. I could leave all my guns at Emily's and just relax. It's nice to be somewhere you're not known.

Soon as Woody and I met the Mexicans and scored more dope, we parted ways again. We both got a half-pound a piece.

I dropped a couple ounces off to Kirby on my way to Havasu. WheI finally made it back to Emily's, I was exhausted. I fell right to sleep. For the past couple of months, I'd been running amok.

When I woke up the following morning, I received a call from Renee. She said this guy went to buy food with her money but instead took the money and never returned. I was in Orange County when it happened. As I'm listening, I'm putting a half of gram of meth inside of a piece of toilet paper, so I can swallow it. Once I washed it down with some water, I replied,

"Renee, this guy is an idiot. I'll be over there with Evil in a half an hour."

Renee told Evil and I where this guy lived, and my ears were ringing from all the meth I ate. My vision was blurry too. I look over at Evil writing down directions to this guy's pad.

"Chris," Evil says, "This guy's pad is next to Tony's."

I lit a smoke and felt for my gun that was tucked into my waistband.

"Chris," he added, "Are you alright homeboy?"

I stood up and replied, "I've never felt better." And walked out the door with my ears still ringing.

When we finally arrived at this guy's apartment the sun was just setting. Lake Havasu nights are great. We didn't even knock on his door, "Hey Chris. How's it going?"

"Good." I replied, "Do you wanna smoke some Meth?"

As we're sitting on his couch getting high, and somewhat having a good time. I start throwing out little hints about the food money he burned Renee for. Then this guy said the funniest thing.

"You guy's ain't here to get me high, are you?"

We took everything of value this guy had, which wasn't much. It didn't have anything to do with the money. I just wanted him to feel what it was like to be burned. When I first started running the streets, I was scandalous too. I learned the same lesson more than once.

"Oh and you need to apologize to Renee."

Evil and I were out the door with at least a hundred CDs and some other crap. We went straight back to Emily so I could prepare for the trip to Pocatello, Idaho. Chucky was calling me almost every hour, "What's up, Dawg! When are you coming?"

# CHAPTER 15

Somewhere in my corrupted mind I thought it would be wise to drive all the way to Idaho with a fully loaded AK -47, bulletproof vest, and several ounces of meth on the back seat covered with a towel.

When I paroled in 2002, I had every intention of being a responsible citizen yet that all came to an end within a few months. My family had no idea where I was, and I was too far gone to care. I was so used to being a criminal that I didn't care about anything. My family was my homeboys, and I was consumed once again with the street way of life. But now, after sitting in prison for several years, it had conditioned me to be a wiser criminal. I even started thinking about holding court on the streets. Meaning I would shoot it out with the cops if they surrounded me. I kept those thoughts to myself, knowing I would be talked out of it.

On the way to Idaho Emily and I stopped in Las Vegas. I just had to try the Blackjack table. Emily just sat and watched. The dealer was acting like a jerk. I grabbed my cards too soon once, and he got all bent out of shape, "you do that again and you'll be sorry!'"

I was spun out with a Glock 45 down my pants, thinking *You stupid idiot. You have no idea!*

By this time, I was not in my right mind again. I simply lost control and all my actions were fueled by meth, which is dangerous.

I was sick and tired of listening to this blackjack dealer. I had already won $500, so I felt good. I just smiled at the dealer and walked off with my cash.

My Uncle Ryan called me as we're leaving for Idaho. I explained to him what I was doing. I couldn't lie to him. And when I hung up the phone, I felt terrible. My thoughts were that I would rather die on the streets than face my family from jail. I respected Uncle Ryan, more than anyone in my family. He's the only reason anyone came to visit me in prison and that meant a lot.

Talk about an awesome drive. Driving to Idaho was something that I would never forget. We arrived safe and relieved.

Chucky had his buddy there waiting to sell my dope for me. I ordered pizza, bought beer, and kicked back. I ended up sleeping most of the time there. I'd wake up with Chucky saying, "Chris, here's $500 more. Where's the dope at?"

His buddy was selling quarter ounces for $500 all day. I was paying less than that for an ounce. Chucky and I were crime partners in the 90s, and I trusted him more than anyone.

Chucky's furniture was in bad shape, so I came up with an idea to purchase new furniture for his pad. Since I was able to make California IDs, I'd rent all new furniture and never return it.

While we're all at this rental place that had furniture, appliances, and things of that nature, I walk up to the cashier and explain I'm starting a business and would like to rent out some furniture for my apartment. I had a stolen checkbook and phony ID. I dressed nice to look the part as well, button down shirt & nice pants. As we're at this place, all spun out on meth, I get this terrible feeling. This guy at the cash register takes to long talk to the manager.

"Chucky," I whispered, "Let's get out of here! Something ain't right."

We take off out the door. When we get to the car I couldn't find my keys. I'm looking all over when Chucky yells, "Chris, they're in the tion."

I pulled out y gun and shot the window out.

Chucky remarked, "Dawg, your still crazy as hell, huh?" We all jumped in the car and sped out of the parking lot.

All in all, Idaho was fun. After that incident, I stayed in Chucky's apartment until leaving for Havasu. The day we left I explained to Chucky that I would be back in a week or two. I could make waymore money out here than Orange County. Plus, I'd be less likely to get busted in Idaho.

By the time we got back to Lake Havasu, Evil had been arrested. He was scaring Tony, the guy who was selling meth for me. I was mad as hell to hear the news. Evil followed me to Havasu, to stay out of trouble and then gets arrested. Now I'm going to have to figure something out with Tony. It never ends.

The first thing I did was go to Richard, "Hey, Richard. I'm glad Evil got busted. He was driving me crazy. I couldn't afford to have him around all the time. Do you know how the cops found him?"

Richard walks into his bathroom as I'm sitting in his chair, "No, Chris. The cops just showed up, knocking on my door." Richard must think I'm ignorant.

Later that day I took Brooke shopping for school clothes. It felt good to be able to buy clothes for her. I took photos of her standing by this little ride in front of the store. I even bought a safe while we were there.

I took Brooke to lunch, then dropped her off at home. I wanted to go visit Richard and try and put a plan in motion to rob him. Actually, the mindset I was in at that time, I wanted to bury him in the desert. But I'd never get away with it. Everyone knew that Evil and I were friends, and they would link it to me.

While Richard and I were smoking meth, I explained to

him about this safe I'm selling, and he bit right into it, "Chris, I'll buy that safe from you." Richard replied.

I hit the pipe with a flame and watched the meth melt, then started smoking and took a big hit. As I blew out the smoke I muttered, "You know what Richard, I'll sell it to you."

I went out to my car and grabbed it off my back seat. Richard having all his valuable possessions in that safe would make it easier to rob him. Especially since I would be by myself. Richard really thought I didn't like Evil. I'd wait a couple weeks, and then when Richard wasn't home, I'd break into his pad and take the safe. I'd sell everything and put the money on Evil's books.

Later I went back to Emily's. As usual I unloaded my car. As I'm laying all my guns on Emily's bed, along with the bulletproof vest and ammo, Michele gave me a weird look. My plan with shooting it out with the cops was looking easier every day. Surely, I didn't want to spend the rest of my days in prison.

"Chris," Michele asks, "Why are you carrying all those guns around with you?"

I popped the clip out of my AK -47 and threw it on the bed "Nothin, just putting them away."

"Yeah, sure Chris," Michele replied.

"What're you trippin' on Michele?"

Right then Emily walked in. Now both were on me. They went on and on about Brooke, saying that I would be leaving her behind if I went to prison forever. Little did they know I wasn't planning on going to prison at all.

After twenty minutes of being guilted into seeing the light, I recalled the conversation with my uncle Ryan. I started hearing all these people say how I'd been messing up. I'm not even sure how to explain it. But Michele could always do that to me. Even when I was with girls she didn't like.

"Chris," Michele would say, "That new girl you're with is not your type." Then two days later I would leave that girl. She was good at that.

After they were done, I promised Michele and Emily that I

would take all my guns and leave them in Orange County, putting them in my storage unit. Then I'll take one more trip to Idaho, and turn myself in. I had plenty of money at this point.

"You promise Chris?" Michele cried.

"I promise Michele."

They somehow made me realize that I was heading for a disaster. The following morning, I packed my car with all my guns and said, "I'm holding onto my Glock-45 until I turn myself in."

Emily and Michele just looked at me like I was stupid. I smiled and headed for home.

As I drove towards Desert Center, I was still trippin' on Evil being locked up in jail. His bail was now two hundred thousand dollars. I'd have to rob a bank to get him out, and that wasn't going to happen.

When I was halfway to Desert Center, I pulled over to shoot off the AK -47. I grabbed it off my back seat and walked a little ways into the desert. On a long stretch of Rice Road there was a railroad track that ran parallel. Teenagers coming and going from Spring Break always stopped to write their names with rocks on the side of the railroad tracks. I'm not sure how they did it, but you could clearly see names on the sides of the tracks as you passed by.

I thought about when Chucky, Kristle, and I drove out to Lake Havasu in the 90s. We stopped on this road because I wanted to paint my name on Rice Road. When we stopped at Desert Center to gas up and eat I reached in my pocket and all my money was gone. I lost over a thousand dollars. I was mad as hell, especially since it was Chuckey's cash.

As soon as I was out of sight I fired away with my AK-47. Talk about a powerful gun. This gun was definitely evil. I went through about 30 rounds in seconds. When I finished, I walked back to my car, loaded the clip again, set it back on the seat, and was on my way to Orange County.

The whole time I'm driving I'm trying to get in contact with Woody. I can't get in contact with him. I started to worry, so I left a message, "Woody. It's me Hinkerton. Call me as soon as you get this message."

How I got the nickname Hinkerton, I'm not totally sure, but it was something that stuck with me and close friends. I never left my real name when leaving a message. So I started using Hinkerton.

A few hours later I drove into the driveway at my pad in Orange. It was still dark, and I noticed a light on in the garage. My 1971 TransAm was parked in there. As I got closer, I heard a noise inside, so I pulled out my Glock-45 and slowly opened the door. I yelled, "What the hell are you doing in here."

This tall skinny looking tweeker looks up with his eyes wide open, "Wo, hey, calm down." This guy replies.

Again, I ask, "What are you doin messing with my car?"

"Kirby is paying me to sand and paint it."

"Oh yeah," I replied, "I forgot about that. Where's Kirby?"

"I think he's sleeping inside of the house."

"Look, I'm sorry. You wanna get high?"

This tweeker looks at me with this weird Look, then replies, "Uh, yeah. Sure. Just as long as you don't shoot me."

I walked towards the house as the tweeker followed me. I held the door for this dude and asked, "What's your name?"

"Russel."

"Russel, wait in the living room, I'll just be a second."

As I walk into the kitchen I yelled to Russel, "Hey, are you hungry?"

"No Chris, I'm good."

Then I walked into Kirby's room, "Kirby, get UP!" I yelled.

"Chris, get out of here." Kirby cried.

I look around at Kirby's messy room, and say, "No, you must get up. We have a lot of things to do. I'll only be here a few days."

My whole plan is to stay in Orange County for two days max then get back to Lake Havasu. I'm sure the sheriffs who busted Dakota are looking for me along with the parole department. I have to be careful.

"Kirby," I said, "where is all the money?"

Kirby sat up rubbing his eyes, and mumbled, "It's in the

safe inside of the closet." I opened the closet and knelt down to open the safe, "Has everyone paid?"

"No," Kirby replied, "Sueann and John still owe, again." I grabbed a couple thousand dollars out of the safe and stood up, "When was the last time you talked to them?"

"Yesterday morning." Kirby muttered, "Are we goin' to get high or what?"

As I sat on Kirby's chair inside of his room I opened my black bag and pulled out a couple of grams.

"Russel... come in here." I yelled. "Oh, I almost shot your buddy, Kirby. I thought he was stealing something."

Kirby grabbed the dope and told Russel to sit down. "At least he didn't beat you up like my other friend. My buddy was inside of his car xing Chris's stereo and Chris seen the light on in his car and ran outside with Evil. Again... Chris thought someone was stealing something, so he beat him up. Then Evil socked him too."

Russel hit the pipe and replied, "Well... he scared the shit out of me with that big ass gun!"

We all sat around smoking meth. I couldn't wait to get back to Lake Havasu. I was getting bad feelings being in Orange County.

By the time I left the sun was just rising. I grabbed all my cash and headed to my storage unit of Glassell, then headed to Woody's pad.

When I pulled into my storage unit, I popped the trunk to grab a blanket. I didn't want anyone or a camera to see me load guns into my storage unit. It wasn't in my name, but still.

I hauled the AK -47, bulletproof vest, and some unnecessary stuff I had lying around into the storage unit, locked it up and left with my Glock-45. I never went anywhere without it.

Woody and I pulled up to his pad at the same time.

"Where have you been homeboy?"

"Spending time with my girl," Woody replied, "Come inside and we'll call the Mexicans."

I followed Woody inside. He rented a room from this lady

after he paroled. We'd both been out of prison for about six months now. The room he rented in Santa Ana was actually nice considering the area. His room was right in front of the house, so he could see who was driving up to his pad.

"I'm only staying in Orange County for a few days Woody. Then I'm going back to Lake Havasu, and from there I'm driving back to Idaho."

After we met the Mexicans, I shook Woody's hand and headed to my cousins Jeremy's, in Mission Viejo. I started hanging out with him a lot ver the past several months. Not only was his house a safe place for me, but I enjoyed his company.

At first when I paroled Jeremy kept drugs away from me. Then I started using and selling meth. Which he wanted no part of in the beginning, but over time he gave up. So I would hang out there.

Jeremy was on his computer when I came through the door. "Christopher, What's up?" Jeremy asked as I walked in.

"Not much. Can you rent me a hotel room?"

Jeremy stood  lit a smoke, "Where do you want a hotel room at?"

I looked out hisedroom window and thought, "How about somewhere with freeway access."

Jeremy grabbed his keys and headed for the door.

Soon as Jeremy left I went into his garage to look at my motorcycle. I kept my GSXR 750 in his garage. It was too easy to steal.

As I'm wiping down all the chrome on my bike I started trippin' on all the memories I have in this house. Good times.

As I'm waiting for my cousin to return, I received a call from Kristle, "Chris, I just got a call from Jay inside the county jail. He was in some motel room that was raided by the police. He's busted again."

"Are you serious," I replied, "I was supposed to pick him up."

"Yeah," Kristle replied, "He mentioned that. Well he's going back to prison."

I lit a smoke and said, "Tell him I'll send him some money, okay?" And I hung up the phone.

I sat there looking out of the garage door, wondering when I'd be back in jail. My thoughts suddenly changed when I received another call from Kirby,

"Chris, it's me Kirby. Sueann and John called. They'll be here in 45 minutes."

"Okay," I replied, "Tell them I'm on my way and not to leave."

"Alright Chris."

Jeremy drove up seconds later. "Here's your room key."

"Thanks Jeremy. I have to go."

As I walking to my car Jeremy yells, "Christopher, would you like to know where your room is located?"

I stopped and said, "Oh man, that might help, huh? I've got so much crap to do that I can't think straight."

"Well," Jeremy replied, "It's at the Embassy Suites, off the 55 freeway. Room 2011."

"Thanks Jeremy," I mumbled.

I headed for the toll road which would be the quickest way back to Orange.

When I pulled into Kirby's driveway, I parked behind John's van and headed inside. I also wanted to remove all of my belongings from this house. Being around this pad was asking for trouble.

"Hey John," I said as I came through the front door. "I need you to help me take some things to my storage unit." John said he had no other place to be, and we started loading up his van.

As we're loading everything into his van I told him that I would gone for at least seven days. And from now on he could take care of Sueann. I had too much other crap to deal with when I came back to this city.

After John and I locked up my storage unit I heard my phone ringing inside of my car. So I ran to answer it, "Hello."

"Chris," Christy cried, "Woody got busted by the cops and I don't know what to do."

Christy is Woody's girlfriend. I've seen her around

throughout all my years running the streets. She's a beautiful girl, to say the least.

"How'd Woody get busted, Christy?"

Through her crying she replied, "The cops raided his room. I think it was the lady who lived there."

"I can't believe this crap, why are you still there Christy?" I asked.

"I'm moving his things to storage. Woody told me to call you. He really needs to talk to you."

I took a seat in my car and lit a smoke, "Do you remember where Kirby lives?"

"Yeah, Chris."

"Meet me there tomorrow morning. I'll call you when I am on my way."

"Thanks Chris."

I couldn't believe it. Almost every one of us was busted. Dakota was pulled over in my car. Luckily I took my motorcycle that day, or I'd already be in jail.

I explained to John that I would see him in a week, and we parted ways.

The following two days were hectic. I literally ran all over Orange County. At the same time, telling myself the whole time that I had to get out of this state. The Anaheim Angels had just won the World Series. All kinds of people were still out front of the stadium. Talk about chaos. Gang bangers were causing all sorts of trouble all over the city. I was just trying to leave and get back to Havasu.

I met Michele over at her place and gave her some dope. Then went to go meet up with Pat in Yorba. Pat is a friend of Woody's. We've only known each other for a couple of months. Now that Woody was in jail we'd be seeing a lot more of each other.

Woody wanted me to help him pay for his lawyer, which I figured would cost $10 thousand. The thing that worried me was who would pay for my lawyer when I got busted. I shook those thoughts out of my head, thinking that I'm being way too careful to be caught slipping.

When I left Michele's to head to Pat's friend's shop, I was in a hurry. I flew down the 57 freeway. I had so much to accomplish before I went back to Havasu. When I got off the freeway, I made a right. With a Glock 45 down my pants and three ounces of meth. A cop pulled right behind me. My heart started pounding in my chest. Next thing I know the cop hit his gas and flew by me. Bringing my heart back to a normal rate of speed. All I wanted to do was light a smoke at this point.

When I pulled into Pat's buddy's shop, he was waiting for me. The shop door was open. This place was cool. I drove inside and Pat introduced me to his buddy.

His name was Kevin. They were all involved with forgery, bank statements, and running stolen checks. These people could literally steal your whole life with your social security number. They'd drain your bank account, cash your bonds, and wreck your life.

Ten minutes after I arrived Tiny called me, "Chris, Where you at?"

I replied, "Where you at?"

"I'm at a hotel off Orange Thorpe and the 57 freeway."

"Can you meet me?" I asked, "A cop just followed me off the freeway. I need you to follow me back to the freeway."

"Yeah, I can do that," Tiny explained, "I'll call you when I get off the freeway."

While I waited for Tiny, I gave Pat a thousand dollars for Woody's lawyer and talked to Kevin about computers. This guy was a genius with computers. After a short discussion, I decided to leave my computer with him. I always carried a laptop with me in my backpack. Kevin said he would download some software that I could use: Windows paint, and some other stuff.

When Tiny called as he was exiting the freeway, I told Kevin I would come by later and pick up my computer. We shook hands and I got in my car. As I pulled out into the alley, I spotted Tiny and his girlfriend. She was driving her SUV. I followed them to the freeway. I didn't wanna take any chances because I didn't know the streets that well in this area. For all I knew the cops were watching Kevin's shop.

Tiny and his girlfriend followed down the 57 freeway, and we exited onto Orange, and made a left right into a Denny's parking lot. Their hotel was right behind Denny's. Since we were all hungry, we decided to have something to eat before going to the hotel.

A few months before I almost stabbed Tiny with a screwdriver, and now we're eating together like nothing happened. The streets never failed to amaze me.

After we ate we went to the hotel and started smoking meth. I discovered we were in Tina's room, another girl I met through Pat. Tina explained to me that she had to rent another room. And that's when I told her she could stay at mine. Usually, I'd never do this in other situations, but I made an exception this time.

Woody's girlfriend rented me a room at the Portofino Suites. I didn't even use the room my cousin rented me because I didn't wanna drive all the way there. This part of Anaheim is usually crawling with police. Because Disneyland is right down the street, so you can imagine all the tourists the police look out for.

After an hour of sitting in their hotel I left. My phone was ringing like crazy. The sun was setting and I wanted to get back to my room. I shook hands with Tiny and said goodbye to the girls, then walked out the door.

All I wanted to do at this point was take care of my business in Anaheim and get back to Havasu, then go to Idaho. Then when I was done making a bunch of money I would turn myself in for my parole violation, before I got busted like the rest of my homeboys.

I arrived at my room and I took a shower. I felt all dirty from driving around all day. When I stepped out of the shower my phone rang.

"Chris, it's me Tina. I'm in the garage at the hotel. Can you help me bring my stuff in?"

"I'll be right there." I put my pants on and a shirt, grabbed my Glock 45 and headed for the door. Tina was good at making money with her checks and things of that nature. So we both had something in common. Who doesn't like to make money? Plus, Tina was nice to look at.

When I stepped into the underground parking lot, I saw Tina with a ten gallon Tuff crate. I grabbed the crate and carried it back to my room.

"Tina," I asked, "what's in this crate?"

"It's blank checks, credit reports, and some other items," Tina replied.

"Sounds confusing to me. Why don't you just sell dope?"

"Too much work, Chris. That's your job."

When I opened the door, I dropped the crate and went into the back room. This hotel was like an apartment, two bedrooms and a living room.

On October 29, 2002, I was walking through the hallway into the living room in thesuite I had rented and thought to myself, *I can't believe I'm staying at this hotel for the second night in a row. I'm pressing my luck. I've gotta get out of Anaheim*

In my bedroom on the dresser was a pocket-tech digital scale. Numerous 4.5 and 2x2 bags to hold meth. Along with one half gram of meth on a plate. In the living room was all of Tina's stuff including a large plastic container with numerous bank statements, birth certificates, and saving bonds.

"Chris," Tina says, "I'll be back in a few hours. I have to take a couple of bank statements to my friend."

"Okay, take the key card on the table. I won't be here when you return. Don't open the door for anyone and remember, Do not tell anyone where I'm staying."

"I won't Chris. Stop trippin'!"

Tina walked out the door without another word. I had just finished weighing out several ounces of meth, and a few grams for my friends. I had to deliver all this dope and get back to my hotel room to meet my connection, before 10 PM tonight. I wanted to be back on my way to Lake Havasu, Arizona before the sun rose in the morning. I'd been having a terrible feeling something bad was going to happen.

I placed all my dope in a little black bag, grabbed my cellphone, put my Glock 45 down my pants, picked up my backpack, and was out the door. Before opening it I looked through the peephole, just to make sure the coast was clear, and with my hand under my shirt holding my gun I opened the door and stepped out into the hallway. I looked from one end of the hallway to the other. Feeling at ease I relaxed and headed for the underground parking garage. As I stepped into the garage, I placed my hand back on my gun until I scanned the parking lot, looking for any hinky individuals. There was no one around except a whole bunch of empty parked cars.

So, I headed for the Ford Explorer I had rented the day before. As I was opening the door a family obviously on vacation was driving trying to find a parking spot. I climbed inside of the Ford, placing my backpack on the passenger's seat, gun on my lap, then started the car. As I drove up the ramp into the ground floor parking lot tourists filled the parking lot. The full moon lit up the sky and I was starting to feel a lot better. All those terrible feelings about something bad happening had stopped. I lit a smoke as I drove to the main street.

When I arrived a Harbor Boulevard, I looked both ways. The traffic was thick. I drove along and arrived at the red light at Lewis and Katella, there was a police car in the right-hand lane on Lewis St. The police car shined a spotlight on me, so I made a right on Lewis, and a quick left into the gas station. All of a sudden, unmarked police cars raced into the gas station, practically surrounding me. I looked from one officer to another thinking, *Son of a bitch! I've got two strikes, a Glock on my lap, a grip of meth, and four police officers staring at me through their windshields.* I looked from one officer to another, and then pushed my gas pedal all the way to the floor. The cops had left enough room to get through their cars. As I flew through I barely missed them.

I made a right back onto Katella going Eastbound, not slowing down for much. I was weaving in and out of traffic at a high rate of real careful not to hit anyone. Because if struck someone while driving it meant another life sentence. Knowing I had to dump all these drugs and gun I had in my possession. I decided to ditch the car in the back of an apartment complex.

Before I even stopped the car I grabbed my backpack and gun and hit the emergency brake, jumping out before it even stopped. I dashed for the first fence I saw, hoping it into an unknown backyard. I could already hear the police helicopter speeding towards my location. The backyard I landed in had a swimming pool so I started dumping bags of meth into the pool. Before I could finish, I could hear footsteps and police officers yelling, "He went over the wall!"

I jumped back on my feet, running through the yard, and leaped the next fence, landing right in front of a pit bull. I quickly jumped over the wall the same way I came. I ran back through the yard with the pool, hopping the next wall into their neighbor's backyard. Soon as my feet hit the ground the helicopter's searchlight lit up the moonlit sky, extinguishing all hopes of my getaway. So as I ran through the next backyard I threw what little dope I had left away. Unfortunately, I still had the Glock 45 in my possession, which I could not get caught with. I really had to think quickly at this point. I climbed one foot in front of the other as I walked on a brick wall trying to keep my balance. A tree overlapped the wall. So as soon as the helicopter's spotlight stopped shining directly onto me, I balanced the gun on a branch, jumped off the wall back onto my feet, running again. I came to a side gate, opened it and started running. I turned the corner and ran into police officers all screaming the same thing, "GET THE FUCK DOWN!" Looking down the barrel of several guns and with nowhere else to run. I got face down.

*SON OF A BITCH! I'm going back to prison.*

# CHAPTER 16

On Aug 1, 2003, I was sentenced to 28-to-life - 3 strikes.

During my second time in prison, what didn't work for me through all those years was doing the same thing, thinking there would be a different result, which was using drugs. I started doing self-help groups at Soledad St. prison in 2012. Narcotic anonymous broke barriers and mentored young kids who came inside the prison. While I was still using drugs, I was on methadone for pain. Saying it's prescribed by the doctor, so it's okay was totally minimizing the situation. I was still using drugs. I wasn't taking any of my self-help classes seriously, which is called half stepping.

After leaving Soledad, I went to VSP, where I succeeded and failed. I successfully completed an electrical vocation but failed miserably in the end. I told myself I was going to take time off from self-help classes to concentrate on my education. Obviously, I didn't pay attention to any of the programs I was enrolled in at Soledad. First off, an addict must stay involved with the program, N.A, or put his sobriety in jeopardy. I started hanging with people who were using meth and ended up selling it on the yard. It was like the streets all over again.

I was again lost in my addiction and ended up in ag-sed, (the hole) on Dec 27, 2015. I woke up in the hole on my daughter's birthday, feeling totally guilty and ashamed for my actions once again. I was fed up with all the drugs. I just couldn't do it anymore. I had to figure out what was going on in my mind to figure out what was going on in my life.

I decided to fully commit to self-help at my next destination. I sought out everyone who was serious about their recovery - drugs, gangs, etc.

I immersed myself in all the new groups CDCR had to offer. N.A, Victims impact, Houses of Healing, C.G.A, the college program, and several other programs.

Once I arrived at High Desert State Prison, I was placed in c-status for 6 months which is a punishment for breaking the rules. They pretty much just lock in your cell for 20 hours a day. That gave me a lot of time to think about my life. Once I was off c-status, I joined C.G.A, (Criminal Gangs Anonymous). I learned all sorts of useful tools that changed my life.

The lifestyle of addiction is when criminals get addicted to committing crimes, and it excels into dangerous territory, such as using guns, robbing people, etc. I now understand that the drugs were not the only problem for me. I fed off being a criminal and what came with that lifestyle.

I also took a victims impact course that helped me understand the cause and effect of crime. When you commit a violent crime, even a non-violent crime, you're affecting a person's life in several ways - emotionally, financially, and physically. You're affecting the first responders who have to save a person's life from the violent crime, the community is affected, and most importantly the families of the victim. That terrifying phone call they receive about their family member being shot, not wanting to go outside because of the fear of what could happen to them. It's a domino effect.

My favorite course was House of Healing. What I got out of it is you must deal with your childhood trauma. If you don't, it will control you in several ways. I held resentment against my dad for starting me on cocaine. I blamed him for everything wrong in my life. It was just an excuse to keep failing. I had to stop blaming everyone else for my actions. I was the problem. I was totally responsible for my life. Until I figured that out, I couldn't move forward. High Desert changed my life. Those courses helped me realize I could change. I could be a good person, a pro-social person. I now possessed the tools I needed to succeed. And I didn't look back.

I joined the college program and quit making excuses for why I couldn't learn. I earned an AA degree. It took 5 years, but I did it.

Then all of a sudden, the laws started changing for non-violent 3 strikers. California passed a law called Prop 57. Non-violent 3 strikers had a chance at parole. I was given a board date. I couldn't believe it. I was notified 6 months before my hearing. My hearing date was set for September 11, 2022. I didn't believe I would be found suitable. But I learned everything I could to hopefully succeed. I had changed my life years before I knew this was coming.

Preparing for the board was the most difficult and stressful thing I ever went through. It's like fighting for your life. Nobody wants to die in prison. I gave it my all. I knew I had a slight chance since I had already changed my life. But you still doubt yourself. Insecurities are a major part of a drug addict's life. If it wasn't for the support network in prison (meaning inmates who strive to become better people), who knows what would of become of me? I learned so much from lifers who would never get out. They told their stories to help the next man.

The California Department of Corrections and Rehabilitation (CDCR)'s Board of Parole Hearings (BPH) is responsible for paroling incarcerated individuals who have been sentenced to indeterminate life terms of incarceration. Historically parole through the BPH process has been difficult due to the political landscape and tough on crime eras of the 1980s and 90s. It took landmark court rulings in legislation

(2008) to put into place the "rational nexus" between incarcerated persons commitment offense and their current behavior. Then the person is no longer considered dangerous. Suitability to parole means the inmate does not pose a current reasonable risk of danger to society.

However, getting to a place where a person is no longer seen as dangerous and suitable to parole is a long journey that takes true change in a person's thinking, attitudes, beliefs, and their behavioral patterns. For many, beginning a lifetime sentence of incarceration is overwhelmingly full of hopelessness and desperation. It often leads to feelings of rejection, bitterness, and deep anger. It takes many years to work through these negative feelings before a person is ready to embark on the self-reflective journey needed to become a successful person at BPH.

The BPH process is like the ultimate job interview. Just like a job interview, a person must put together a resume about themselves called a portfolio.

The biggest obstacle was putting together a complete parole packet. Insight paper, relapse prevention plans, essays, laudatory Chronos, and a copy of all your accomplishments through the years. Luckily, I took advantage of these during my time in prison. I completed 3 vocations and earned an AA degree and a business entrepreneurship certificate. The vocations I successfully completed were Office Services, Janitorial, and Electrical. Today I only use one, the electrical vocation. Completing a viable trade was the best thing I could have done because I now have a great job working as an electrician.

In addition to putting together a portfolio, a person will have two important interviews before a decision is reached in whether the person is suitable for parole or unsuitable for parole. The first interview is a psychological evaluation four months prior to your parole hearing by a psychologist employed by the BPH's Forensic Analysis Division (FAD). The second is the parole hearing itself. It will be held by two BPH commissioners resulting in either a grant, or a denial of parole.

The real preparation for the BPH should start once a person is sentenced to any life term. The focus needs to be on self-improvement endeavors in a wide variety of topics including education, vocational trades, substance abuse, recovery, mental health, emotional literacy, cognitive behavioral intervention, and learning coping skills and tools to help a person deal with many hardships incarceration causes. Ideally, a person stays busy throughout their sentence pursuing self-improvement in preparation of their parole hearing. If a person is not doing so already, it is critical they immediately begin to evolve themselves in rehabilitative programming with the intent of understanding how they became a person capable of committing a violent crime acts in society.

The BPH is looking for several factors in their decision when a person comes before the board. However, the most important aspect is who this person is before them today. While a person's whole life will be reviewed, with a focus on the committed offense which brought that person to prison, their focus will ultimately be on the person today. This is when the term: insight becomes the most important aspect of the hearing. Insight in a hearing means the person understands all the factors that went into committing a violent act. With insight a person is seen as taking responsibility for, and becoming accountable to, their behavior which broke the laws of society, thereby harming people and society itself. When these aspects are present in a person, they are viewed as having remorse and regret for their harmful actions. By achieving this state through actively participating in rehabilitative programming and self-improvement, it endeavors a person to be making amends. Living in amends is proof that the person before BPH has become pro-social- a law-abiding person.

Leading up to a parole hearing a person must begin to work on their portfolio and the topics they need to discuss with the parole commissioners at the hearing. A solid portfolio will include many documents which showcase a person's clear understanding of their negative lifestyle, how it led to the crimes they committed, what caused their change into a more positive person, how they will remain this changed individual, and what are their future plans after incarceration.

The order of parole hearings never change. First, the commissioner will lead a conversation about a person's life from birth to committed offense. Next, the other commissioner will review everything the person has done since their incarceration has begun. This discussion will also review parole plans and many questions on how the person expects to live in society. The commissioners will want to know how hardships will be coped with. Both the D.A. and the incarcerated attorney will have an opportunity to ask questions of them. Directly following these questions are the closing statements. These are by the DA, the incarcerated person, or, the victims, or the victim's next of kin. After these statements, the commissioner will go into recess to discuss their decision concerning suitability.

If a person is granted parole, a review is conducted by the BPH, for 120 days, and the Governor has 30 days to review the decision after the BPH. If the person is denied parole, the commissioners will determine the next parole hearing. Denial lengths are 3, 5, 7, 10, and 15 years.

The central question of a parole hearing is to find out who the person is today. If the person is no longer seen as a danger to society, then they are to be released. The person can come in front of the board many years, often decades after their offense was committed. These years are used to truly understand everything that went into the person becoming capable of committing the crime. A person who reaches this place no longer lives in shame of their past. They can see clearly who they are today is no longer the person they were. This is a then and now perspective. They now accept responsibility for the devastation they caused to a vast number of people, and to society. This is insight on a deeper level. What it takes to be successful at the BPH is a willingness to come before those who have suffered harm, take responsibility for the impact of destructive, violent, and criminal acts, and take accountability through honoring the victims and survivors by living a life in amends.

I went from never thinking I was never going to get out, to being freed in 2022.

# CHAPTER 17

I have been out of prison for eight months. By the grace of God, there have been no serious obstacles whatsoever. I started working my first two weeks out picking up the trash on the side of the freeway, knowing it was only for a short time. Since I completed an electrical vocation in 2015, that was exactly what I was going to do with my life. Nothing was going to get in my way. I immediately started looking around for a job in the electrical field.

On April 4th, I started with an electrical company, which gave me a chance. Knowing I just got out of prison after serving 20 years, it was touch and go for a few months. Some of the employees were nervous around me. It was difficult to adjust at first. One day my boss said to me, "You have to be more sociable with the guys." I was having trouble relating to any of the guys. But now six months later they appreciate me for my hard work, and I am excelling at the job.

I think what really made me a successful electrician, was all the hard work I did to complete the vocation. I spent 8 hours a day in school for almost 2 years and consumed all the information I could. Another defining factor was I landed a maintenance job at High Desert State Prison. I used all the schooling I was taught. I worked in the boiler room/main laundry for 5 years. I learned how to do HVAC, troubleshoot laundry machines, and work on several other types of machinery. But I think the best part of me is my hard work ethic. Stay busy, and always be grateful for what you have.

# EPILOGUE

So I shared my story, so typical among inmates, living in darkness, to show how negative peer pressure, and broken families, can steer you into the insanity of criminality and the cancer of drug use. That lifestyle is not glamorous. The movies of gangsters and all the songs that glamorize that lifestyle are lies. All I managed to do was destroy y dreams, my freedom, my family, and countless others from my irresponsible and selfish behavior.

I have a son that barely speaks to me. My daughter, who I love very much, is now 27 years old. I only spent 8 months with her when she was 6 years old. Why, because I was either on the run or locked-up. I failed as a father. After getting out of prison for the first time, I met my wife and made a promise to her and myself, that I would stay clean and spend my time with positive people. That lasted 4 months. I made excuses, went back to old friends, and a lifestyle of destruction. In the process I went back to prison and lost my wife.

It comes down to this I was looking for solutions to my broken-down life in all the wrong places. My life was over. I failed everyone. I also failed society by hurting everyone in my path.

I am not making excuses or blaming my family or anyone else. I take full responsibility for all my negative actions and for failing all those who cared for me. Finally, truth and maturity caught up with me. I hit rock bottom I looked for hope and maybe redemption. I started asking for help to change my insane lifestyle, for a chance to live in the light. I know I can never change my past, but maybe I can change my future by living right.

My story that I shared was insanity. Today I am able to change my story into something good by helping others recover and stopping the cycle of victimization. I don't ever want to hurt anyone else, and by sharing my story, maybe someone will see similarities in their own life and find the courage to ask for help to change their stories.

Positive friends that support your interest, help you recover from the drug addiction and the lifestyle that comes with it and education are the keys to a life filled with peace, hope, and love.

Most importantly I have a huge support network. Friends, my daughter, mom, stepdad, and my girlfriend. Most of all I have God on my side. I truly think losing your freedom and thinking you'll never get out of prison changes a person's perception of life.

It's amazing what a person can do with his life if he wants to. No excuses, just the will to succeed. Plus, the groups out here helping paroles with tools, food, housing, and several other necessities, are amazing. Without a lot of those programs, lifers paroling back into society would fail. My friends have had a huge impact on my life since I've been out. All ex-addicts/gang members who now help others get sober, or get them jobs, etc. Make no mistake, an individual must have the will to be a better person. It's like growing up again. You must learn how to be responsible, pays bills, save money, be considerate of others, know when you're in a toxic situation, and most importantly when to ask for help.

I'm just now getting to truly know my daughter Brooke. Who surprisingly doesn't hate me for leaving her out in this world without a dad. She's a grown responsible woman now, but that connection you get being with your child will never be there for us because I wasn't there. My son will barely even talk to me. There is no one to blame but myself. I failed as a citizen, a dad, and a son. Because I was selfish and only cared about myself and drugs. I can finally say that I am not that person any longer. I have compassion, respect for others, and the tools to be a better person. I'm living proof people can change.

Change is possible. It takes courage to raise your hand for help. Hate is easy; that is the coward's way. As humans, we have to stand up together to break the chains of bondage that keeps us locked up in the lies of drugs and criminality. I don't even know what the future holds for me, but I do know that I am firmly planted in the path of making a positive contribution in every way possible.

Today I am a man. I can look at myself in the mirror and see a good man that cares.

I hope and I pray that I will be able to save lives by sharing my story. I have a purpose. I found hope. I'm determined to utilize my life experience in a positive way. No more wearing a mask of a gangster. I'm able to laugh, cry, and care for others. I will fight for change and do all I can to change the lost stories of others into lives that heal and become a positive contributing person to a society that is tired of victimization.

Today I have hope.